prepared to DYE

Dyeing Techniques for Fiber Artists

by Gene Shepherd

RUG HOOKING

Copyright © 2013 by Stackpole Books
Published by
STACKPOLE BOOKS
5067 Ritter Road
Mechanicsburg, PA 17055
www.stackpolebooks.com

www.rughookingmagazine.com

All rights reserved, including the right to reproduce this book or portions thereof in any form or by any means, electronic or mechanical, including photocopying, recording, or by any information storage and retrieval system, without permission in writing from the publisher. All inquiries should be addressed to *Rug Hooking Magazine*, 5067 Ritter Road, Mechanicsburg, PA 17055.

Printed in the United States of America

10 9 8 7 6 5 4 3 2 1

Photographs by the author except where otherwise noted
Cover design by Caroline Stover

Library of Congress Cataloging-in-Publication Data

Shepherd, Gene R.
Prepared to dye / Gene Shepherd.— First edition.
    pages cm
ISBN 978-1-881982-92-0
1. Dyes and dyeing. I. Title.
TT853.S54 2013
667'.3—dc23
2012045795

Acknowledgments

I would never have been prepared to dye were it not for those mentors, friends, and colleagues who have provided me with technical insight, inspiration, and encouragement:
Ginny Brown, Frankie Cagle, Marny Cardin, Helen Coles, Helen Connelly, Jackie Hansen, Sandy Harris, Dorothy Hart, Anne-Marie Littenberg, Harriet Wait Norman, Jane Olson, Diane Phillips, Lisa Rueger, Ann Taylor, Mildred Wheatcroft, Marion Wise, and Patty Yoder.

The impact of this book is far richer due to the artists who used my wool to create wonderful illustrations for each batch of dye:
Elizabeth Black, Donna Bleam, Jean Coon, Karen Cunagin, Susan Feller, Carla Fortney, Teresa Heinze, Bernie Heron, Barbara Holden, Mary Lynn Gehrett, Janet Griffith, Carla Jensen, Peggy Johnson, Phyllis Lindblade, Florence Lipar, Ruth Locke, Jean McEwen, Brigitta Phy, Laura Pierce, Robin Price, Sarah Province, Iris Salter, Alanah Schuck, Penny White, Jan Winter, Marion Wise, and Emily Gail Wyett.

Completing a project like this requires the timely acquisition of special photos, supplies, information, emotional support, and—quite literally—field work, like that provided by:
Charlotte Bell, Rex and Glenna Bunting, Nancy Hill, Susan Madrigal, David and Marilee Pearson, Ann Shepherd, Marsha Shepherd, Kathy St. Ledger, Wilfred and Jean Taylor, Jim White, and the Technical Support Staff at Pro Chemical Dyes.

At the beginning, for embracing this project, in the middle, for sustaining it, and at the end, for making it all come to life in printed form, I acknowledge the dedicated work of Deb Smith, my editor, and the support staff at Stackpole Books.

To all of these people I am both indebted and extremely grateful.

Gene Shepherd, Anaheim, California, 2013

Contents

Acknowledgments iii
Introduction vi

Part One: Getting Started

Chapter 1: Dye Kitchen Tools and Setup 2
Chapter 2: Prepping Fiber before You Dye 14
Chapter 3: Dyeing with Commercial
 Acid Dyes 22

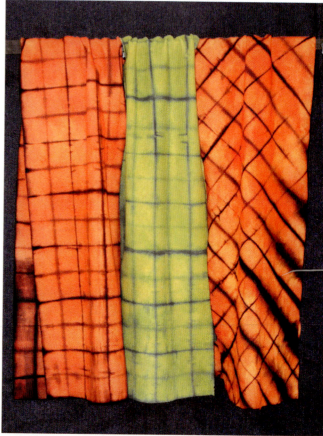

Part Two: Dyeing in Batches

Dyeing with Commercial Acid Dye

Batch 1: Solid Color with No Mottling 26
Batch 2: Solid Color with Mottling 30
Batch 3: Overdyeing Colored Wool 36

Batch 4: Lazy Swatches 45	**Batch 14:** Dyeing Mohair 135
Batch 5: Traditional Multivalue Swatches 53	**Batch 15:** Dyeing Nylon 139
Batch 6: Dip Dyes 60	
Batch 7: Jelly Roll 69	## Dyeing without Dye
Batch 8: Your Own Wheel of Color 74	**Batch 16:** Bleeding Wool 145
Batch 9: Spot Dyes 82	**Batch 17:** Antique Black 156
Batch 10: Dump Dyes 99	**Batch 18:** Marbleized Wool 163
Batch 11: Dyeing for Animals 112	**Batch 19:** Transitional Pieces 176
Batch 12: Stacked Pot 118	**Index of Tips** 184
Batch 13: Ordered Casserole Pancake 124	**Resources** 186

Introduction

WHILE ATTENDING MY FIRST HOOK-IN and after just three weeks of rug hooking, I made this confident prediction: *I'll never fiddle with dyeing my own wool because I can't imagine going through all that hassle.* Just a few months later, I was mixing dye as I stood over four pots of boiling water. As they say, the rest is history.

What made the difference? Initially, two things: necessity and encouragement. While necessity may be the mother of invention, it is also why I started dyeing wool fabric. When my first commission came in a few months after that first hook-in, I learned that I not only needed more beautiful wool than I could afford to buy, I needed wool in colors that I could not find. I had to get a stash of wool, and I had to get it fast. As luck would have it (actually, I think it was more Divine providence than luck) my local rug hooking group from San Louis Obispo County, California, was the best support group that any newbie could ever hope to find. They provided me with the encouragement I needed, along with liberal amounts of information, supplies, wool, and equipment. Before long, they had me so convinced about my potential abilities that I scheduled a dye day at my house based on the promise that several of them would come to help.

I will never forget that first dye session. Four of the ladies showed up early in the morning with all sorts of supplies. Before long, there were boiling pots ready for the first batches of dye and wool. I looked at them and said: "I think you ought to do the first batch and I will just watch. After all, I have never dyed anything at all." The four ladies looked at one another and replied: "We have never dyed either—we've just listened to people talk about it at workshops. You have as much actual experience as we do! Start dyeing."

On that first dye day I learned the third essential ingredient for successful dyeing: courage. If you want to dye fiber, there comes a point where you have to roll up your sleeves, turn up the heat, and start mixing and pouring dye! Sure, it can be risky business. Not every pot turns out the way you envision, and some pots even disappoint. However, if you are willing to push the edges, some pots of dyed fiber surpass your wildest dreams. You just have to be courageous.

Left to right, back row: *Sandy Harris, Marion Wise, Marny Cardin. Front: Frankie Cagle. Without these four ladies and the rest of the SLO Rug Hookers—I would never have had the confidence or motivation to dye my first pot of wool. As luck would have it, my garage had an old working stove—the perfect place to dye.*

Here is proof that I was not only present for that session, but active enough to get my shirt good and wet! While I had forgotten the actual month we met, this photo confirms that we were dyeing shortly before or right after Christmas of 1998. From left to right: Marion Wise, Gene, Frankie Cagle, and Marny Cardin, with Sandy Harris behind the camera.

If *necessity* has brought you to this book, I will encourage you with lots of instructional information, complete with courage boosting tips.

▲ You can easily find good equipment.
▲ You can follow the steps in this book.
▲ You can roll up your sleeves and get to work.

If *I* can do this (Good grief—I am a theologian with an undergraduate degree in vocal performance!), *you* can do this.

Over the years, I have encountered many people who never dye simply because they don't think they have the right setup. While it is true that much money can be spent on space and equipment, it is also true that fabulous stacks of interesting wool can be made in one pot with absolutely no dye at all.

Readers will probably notice that I don't spend much time on detailed color recipes: this is a process book, not a recipe book. It's not that I don't like recipes. There are already many wonderful books on that subject, and I don't think another one from me would be all that helpful. My goal is to help the home dyer by showing how any dye recipe can be used in various different processes, or batches, to make great wool. While all 19 of the batches (and batch versions) demonstrated in this book come with specific instructions, the dye colors for each can be changed to suit your tastes.

I don't use many complicated recipes; I rely on sight as much as on recipe. While that confession may make novice dyers hear warning bells and alarm whistles in their heads, please relax, take a deep breath, and trust me. (After all, if you can't trust your minister, whom can you trust?) There is a sequential order to the lessons in this book. While you can, of course, read them out of order, each batch or lesson lays a knowledge and experiential foundation for the one that follows. Such a foundation will build knowledge, skill, and courage. If you follow through the book in this way, somewhere about midpoint you ought to find yourself slinging dye and making substitutions with abandon because *it just looked like it needed a little something else.* If that is the case, then I will feel like my work has been successful. After all, my goal is to get you to the place where you are prepared to dye!

PART ONE: GETTING STARTED

In this section you'll find everything you need to know about preparing not only yourself, but also your dye space and your fiber for the dye process.

Chapter 1: Dye Kitchen Tools and Setup

One of the goals of this book is to help you be more productive with your space, time, and money. After reading this chapter, you'll be able to set up a safe and successful dye kitchen that is right for you and your budget.

Chapter 2: Prepping Fiber before You Dye

Prepping Fiber Before You Dye gives simple instructions that will allow you to accurately prep and assemble the uniform amounts of fabric and yarn needed for all the projects in this book.

Chapter 3: Dyeing with Commercial Acid Dyes

Dyeing With Commercial Acid Dyes answers many of the questions and myths that surround this subject. Armed with such information, you can start dyeing wool with confidence. I've even provided a list of the dye colors I can't live without to help you get started.

Chapter 1
Dye Kitchen Tools and Setup

Essential Materials for the Dye Kitchen

- Water source
- Heat source
- Pot or pan
- Dye and setting agents
- Measuring spoons and cups
- Stirring spoons
- Sturdy tongs
- Safe place to drain hot water

There was unanimous approval on the day I announced I was taking my dye paraphernalia out of the kitchen to a dedicated dye space. Not only did the family observe a formal day of celebration, they came through with supportive comments like these: Would it help if I started moving equipment now? Here's $5 to speed the process. Will you also take the dye stains from the wooden workspace?

A Good Place to Dye

It really does not take all that much high-tech equipment to dye a batch of wool fabric or fiber. After all, artisans did manage, for a few millennia, to accomplish the task using only a pot, wood fire, natural dyes, and a wooden stick to stir. Of course, on occasion, they also caught their clothes on fire and scalded themselves (or an observer) to death while trying to deal with vats of boiling water.

Fortunately, with all the modern conveniences available today, the home dyer can accomplish a dye session without all those traditional risks. You can set up an effective dye station whether you are working on a shoestring budget or investing a few hundred dollars.

Since water and heat are the two most difficult things to manage in the dye process, pick a place to dye that easily accommodates both.

Your Home Kitchen

The home kitchen is a natural choice since kitchens usually contain a sink and some type of stove or cooktop. Having a ready supply of water in close proximity to a heat source, as well as a place to drain boiling water after dyeing is done, is the ideal setup. Fewer steps taken with pots of water, whether cold or hot, lessens the strain on backs as well as the risks involved with hot liquids. Additionally, stoves and worktops in most kitchens are at the correct height for good work conditions.

Home Kitchen Concerns

While all the dyes I buy are advertised as "safe," none of the manufacturers recommend them for human consumption. And, there are all those vintage packets of good dye that I have bought, inherited, or received as gifts over the years. I mix old dyes with new dyes all the time. Some of those packets are nearly as old as I am. Since I really don't know what each different manufacturer used to make their dyes over the past 60 years, I am pretty skeptical about accidentally mixing my dye equipment with my cooking equipment. Even with the new dyes, it can't be a good idea to mix food and colorfast dye. Bottom line: Don't mix your dye utensils with your food prep utensils. Keep a dedicated set of measuring spoons, measuring cups, pots and pans, and stirring sticks for each.

Then, there is the mess factor. Even when I am incredibly careful, pots boil over, glass measuring cups full of mixed dye break, and wet wool slops and drips at the most inconvenient times and places. It is at those stressful, inconvenient times when I tend to grab the cooking tongs instead of the dye tongs or my wife's measuring cup instead of my dye measuring cup.

Bottom line: The kitchen is a fine place to dye fiber as long as you bring your organizational "A" game.

Patio Dyeing

Because of the potential mess, you may want to find a place outside your kitchen. It is fine to take the dye process outside, but don't settle for hazardous conditions. If you have a sturdy, solid-top patio table, then you may be able to make a good temporary dyeing station any time weather permits. However, don't settle for less than optimum situations.

What is wrong with this picture? Everything! A wicker table is never a good idea for a dye session. I have actually seen one wicker table catch fire with a similar setup as shown in this photo. This particular tabletop is so stretched and bowed down in the middle that it creates a very uneven surface, making the oversized pan and undersized hot plate even more unstable. The coffee-table height makes all aspects of the process—lifting, stirring, and seeing—more difficult. The electrical cord just hangs off the table asking to be snagged as someone passes by. The only thing that could make this setup worse would be for the dyer to be barefooted when the pot unexpectedly boils over!

This sturdy waist-high cart makes an excellent outdoor dyeing station. The top has a lip around the outside edge, helping to contain both the hotplate and any boiling spills that might occur. Additionally, there is enough unused space on the top to lay a few tools and measuring cups, not to mention all the shelf space below. The construction of the cart also provides a way to securely wrap electrical cords to reduce the likelihood of snagging one. Often, carts like this have wheels with locking mechanisms. For those that don't, block the wheels with wedges so the cart cannot move.

While it does not look too pretty, this old Toastmaster plate is my most efficient alternative heat source. Measuring in at about 9½" square, this 1,000-watt plate supports and balances bigger pots better than double burner units do. As I usually want to do bigger rather than smaller amounts, I prefer this burner and a pot to a much smaller electrical/hot pot unit. Additionally, it is easy to store as well as cart around for dyeing road trips.

One would assume that a two-burner unit would produce twice as much power as a single plate. However, most models have different controls and different wattage for the two burners. This particular unit has one 650-watt coil and a 1,000-watt coil. In my experience, the 1,000-watt coil on a double burner never gets as hot as the 1,000-watt burner on my single plate.

Patio Dyeing Concerns

Both weather and a dependable heat source can greatly affect an outdoor dyeing experience. I have used about everything you can think of as a heat source for patio dyeing, and the only thing I can recommend is something with an electrical coil or heating unit instead of a flame.

Where I live, the wind is usually too brisk for a satisfying "flame" dyeing experience. Even when I place windbreaks around the burners there is still too much flickering and heat loss for my tastes. Such inconsistency slows things down more than I can tolerate. Consequently, I stick to electric hot plates and electric skillets/pots for my infrequent patio dye sessions because I know the power will be consistent.

Even with efficient portable equipment, the patio is not my favorite place to dye. However, if that is the best space you can find then, by all means, utilize it to the best of your ability.

A Lesson from Las Rancheritas

The Las Rancheritas Rug Hookers from San Agustin, Mexico, use a simple yet highly effective portable kitchen when dyeing their wool.

The group's dye kitchen heat source is a split-barrel fire pit, built waist high on sturdy legs. It can be positioned on any level outdoor spot. A garden hose, shown in the background, provides the ready water source. As the stove is approachable from every direction, dyers need not scald themselves trying to stir pots on a back row of burners.

Forget about a two-burner hotplate. When this baby is fully (and literally) fired up, nine pots (or buckets) of wool could be cooking at one time! The dyer tending this pot of wool also uses very high-tech equipment for stirring: a stick.

While dyeing over a wood fire may not be everyone's cup of tea, this setup works, and it works very well for both dyeing wool and making a cup of tea. You do not have to spend a lot of money to create a safe and effective dye kitchen.

Photos by Charlotte Bell

TIPS — SUCCESSFUL KITCHEN DYEING

- Cover your workspace with a plastic tablecloth.
- Remove all normal kitchen utensils from the work area so you can't grab the wrong item by mistake.
- Have a dedicated set of pots, measuring cups, and tongs that look different from their kitchen counterparts.
- Cover the floor in your traffic area with old throw rugs that can't be harmed by some spills.
- Get cheap gallon buckets to soak and transfer wool.
- Don't dye at the same time food is being prepared.
- Don't dye when there will be people passing through the kitchen.
- Don't dye when you are in a hurry—give yourself plenty of time.

Dedicated Dye Space and Equipment

Since dedication is a theme all pastors love to preach about, you should not be surprised that I have worked that topic into our basic discussion about dyeing. If you can carve out any sort of a dedicated space to dye fiber, whether it is in your basement, garage, or outbuilding, it will certainly improve your dye experience. Having everything right at your fingertips simplifies the process, and encourages spontaneity—and spontaneity is an important part of the artistic experience.

Here is a prioritized list of things for a dedicated dye space. You do not need to have every item on this list. Any one or a combination of them, however, will improve your experience.

There are three electrical outlets shown in this photo. All three are on separate, dedicated, breakers. (There is actually a fourth dedicated outlet on the other side of this wall, on my patio, so that a fourth station can be set up there or in the studio via an electrical cord running in from the patio.) That means, on this one small table, three or four double hotplates can be fired up at one time without causing an electrical breaker to blow.

1. Plenty of Electricity
If you are limited to plug-in electrical sources of power, then improve that option with as many dedicated electrical outlets as possible.

2. Stainless Steel Worktable
A sturdy workspace is an essential safety item. Imagine the problems should the legs on a plastic folding table give out, causing everything to collapse. I have had that happen—without the boiling water! While there are lots of options, from sturdy wooden tables to kitchen cabinetry and counter-tops, nothing can equal the durability and flexibility of restaurant-grade stainless steel worktables.

Built at the proper work height for the average person, stainless steel tables don't easily stain, strain, melt, collapse, or catch on fire. They do cost more than plastic folding tables. But, in this instance, you certainly get your money's worth for the investment.

3. Oversized Sink
While an oversized sink does not need to be as elaborate as the one shown here, the value of a convenient water source that can easily accommodate large pots cannot be overstated. For much less than the cost of this unit, a plastic janitor's mop sink can serve the needs of the home dyer.

If your sink is too small to presoak much wool, use a couple of busboy tubs. They are relatively inexpensive, stackable, lightweight, and useful for a variety of other things in the dye kitchen. The important thing is to have some sort of sink in which you can easily get and dispose of water.

This three-well stainless steel sink with drain boards was about one-third the cost of the traditional cabinet/kitchen sink setup that I originally planned for this area. By accident, when shopping for stainless steel tables at a restaurant supply store, I saw this sink and thought to myself: Now that would let me soak some wool—pity I can't afford it! Imagine my surprise when I checked the tag and discovered that, in addition to being the more desirable option, it was also the most affordable option.

Each 14" deep well in this commercial sink can soak about 15–18 yards of wool at one time. As I usually don't dye more than that in one session, two wells are still available so that one can be used for draining pots and the other for rinsing wool. Because the sink is positioned next to the heat source, it makes everything easier and safer.

4. Heat Source

Nothing takes the place of a dedicated stove—preferably one with both burners and an oven. If you have a choice, a gas stove is hard to beat because the heat temperature can immediately go up and down with just a turn of the knob. This is a very important feature when a pot is on the verge of boiling over! You do not need a top-of-the-line unit—just something dependable.

Right: *My first stove in this space was our old kitchen stove. After a few years of using that, I found an ancient six-burner commercial stove that I got for a song. Even though that oven never worked very well, the commercial power of the six burners was a wonderful boost to my productivity. When it finally got to the point where it could not be serviced anymore, I traded up to this energy-efficient updated electronic-ignition model that has both topside burners and an excellent oven.*

Far Right: *As proof of the fact that almost any working stove will do, here is a vintage shot of my good friend Jane Olson in her outdoor studio, swatch dyeing on her apartment-sized stove. Few people in their lifetime will ever equal the yardage of dyed wool that Jane did each year on this little gas stove. Take note that her stove is right next to a plastic mop sink and a waist-high worktable. There is nothing fancy about this setup, yet it was one of the most productive dye studios in the United States for many, many years.*

Early in my career, I may have imprinted while watching Ginny Brown and Jane Olson dye in white enamel pots. Consequently, my first dye pot purchases were white enamel pans from antique and thrift stores. Special people have also given me pots and pans over the years, which I treasure and use with great care. No matter how you stack them, white enamel pots take up a lot of space. Still . . . they do look good in any space they occupy!

5. Equipment

Fortunately, after you get some pots and pans, it does not take very many other pieces of equipment to fill out a well-stocked dye lab.

White Enamel Pots and Pans

White enamel pots and pans have long been the gold standard among home dyers. That is true, in part, because the white background allows the color of the dye to show up a little better than other backgrounds do. Since I dye as much in other types of pots as I do in white pots, I must say I don't find the white ones to be that much better than other good options. Still, there is something particularly nice about using good white enamel pots. For me, it is as much about an emotional tie to the utensil as it is anything else.

Though much beloved, these white enamel pots and pans do have some drawbacks:
- They can be hard to find
- They chip very easily (cheap ones more so than expensive ones).
- They stain very easily (bleach works wonders for a few years).
- They take up a lot of space.

Stainless Steel Pots and Pans

Stainless steel pans, like their white enamel cousins, are also non-reactive. For that reason, they are also suitable for use in your dye kitchen. More and more I find myself using stainless steel instead of white enamel.

Part of the reason I gravitate to stainless steel is because restaurant supply stores sell a large variety of pots, pans, and lids in uniform, graduated sizes. If they can stack together on a showroom shelf, they can stack together in a minimal amount of studio space, immediately making them much easier to store than the odds-and-ends sizes of other pans.

It is good to have an assortment of sturdy stainless steel steamer pans like those used in commercial steam tables: shallow pans for baking wool and deeper pans for stovetop simmering techniques. A retired caterer gave all of these pans to me. Getting lids for these old pans was no problem as the standard sizes are all still available at my local restaurant supply house.

If you are looking for stainless steel pans, don't confine your search to restaurant supply houses. These stainless steel pots came from a very cheap discount store. They are the best big pots I have.

Can't find a pan in the size you want? Have a metalworker make it! After fantasizing for months about what I could do with a single pan that fit over four burners, I finally found a metalworker to make one for me. Although it is very close to being too much of a good thing, it comes in handy for some of the large dyeing projects I like to do. I show it simply with the suggestion that you not be limited in your approach to acquiring dye pots and pans.

It makes no difference if it is white, pink, or speckled-blue enamel or stainless steel, a 1-quart saucepan with an easy-to-grip handle is an indispensable tool for transferring extra water and boiling a little extra "mix" water. It's a good mixing/diluting vessel for strong colors and the best way to transfer hot dripping wool from one spot to another.

Dye Spoons

Given the very small amounts of dry dye needed for most recipes, a complete set of dye spoons is essential. While I regularly run into people who try to avoid the cost of this purchase, this is not the place to skimp on good equipment.

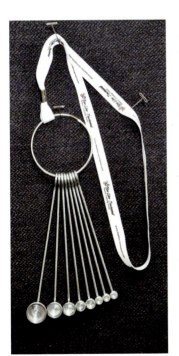

Spoon sets tend to come in two ways: single spoons for each measurement (usually eight different spoons on some sort of ring as with the Bee Line set pictured here) or four spoon shafts with a different measurement on each end. As can be expected, the setup with eight shafts always costs more money than the one with just four shafts. However, after losing several of those independent double spoons, I determined that it was much cheaper in the long run to get the kind where everything stays connected on a big ring. I also find it much easier to locate the specific spoon I want when mixing up a recipe as they are placed in graduated order on the ring.

These are the measurements you need for a good set of dye spoons: 1, $1/2$, $1/4$, $1/8$, $1/16$, $1/32$, $1/64$, and $1/128$ teaspoon.

This straight-edge cup configuration is particularly helpful when scraping off excess dye to get an accurate measurement.

Dye Kitchen Tools and Setup

Measuring Cups

Measuring cups serve double-duty as measuring devices and mixing containers. As some dye applications take multiple colors, plan on having several on your shelf.

After I'd broken a dozen or more glass measuring cups, a friend suggested plastic cups. It did not take long to figure out that this was a wise idea. Besides their durable nature, the handles on plastic cups do not get hot. Additionally, plastic cups stack together much more efficiently than glass, conserving my limited space.

Collect four or five measuring cups each in 1 cup and 2 cup sizes. I buy new plastic measuring cups when I go to the store and I don't pass up cheap ones at garage sales. If you are a prolific dyer, more makes for a merrier big dye day.

Mixing Spoons

Mixing spoons are another indispensable item you need to get in volume.

Common table or soup spoons are perfect for stirring dye solutions or spooning mixed color over wool when spot dyeing small amounts. I also use these spoons to measure generous spoonfuls of citric acid. In this case, any odd stainless steel spoons will do the trick. They can be found for a song at garage sales and thrift stores. My spoons are stored in a plastic commercial dishwasher basket. After cleaning up, all the wet spoons go back in the basket, where they drip dry.

Tongs

Once actual dyeing begins, a good set of tongs will be your most used tool. As not all tongs are created equal, please take care to get the right sort of tongs.

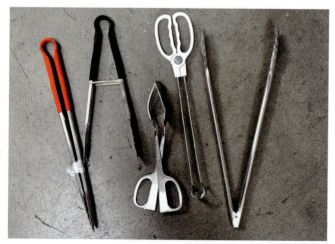

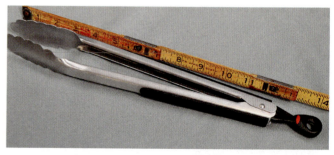

I don't like any of these tongs: the "bent" kind are too wobbly; the scissor kind are too loose; the spring-action kind don't have enough action. If you are handling little pieces of wool, these tongs will work reasonably well. However, as pieces get bigger—¼, ½, and 1 yard—a more substantial tong set is essential.

In my opinion, these OXO brand tongs are the perfect dye tongs. They are long enough at 14" to do double-duty as a pot-stirring device (eliminating the need to switch back and forth between utensils). They also lock at the hinge, which helps the dyer grab and hold a piece of wool, a particularly helpful feature for those of us with arthritis pain in our hands. The ability to grip and hold is essential when moving hot wool from the dye pot, as well as when doing dip dyes. Such tongs allow the dyer to get the final end of the wool much closer to the boiling water than is possible with fingers!

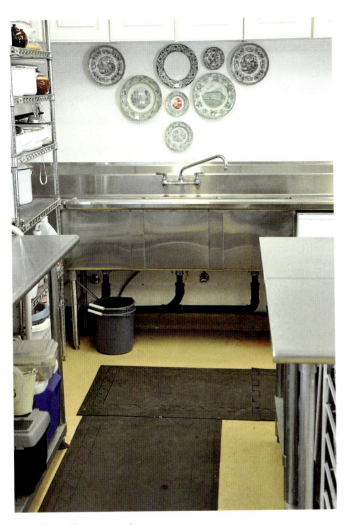

6. Miscellaneous Items

You'll need just a few more items to fully stock your dye lab.

A **kitchen timer** is much better at keeping track of an hour cooking interval than my memory.

Cushioned **floor mats** in the work area are a must. They relieve body stress and provide a nonslick surface.

When setting my wool, I use either **citric acid crystals** (on the left) or **clear vinegar**. As 1 tablespoon of citric acid equals ¾ cup of clear vinegar, citric acid takes up much less space than the vinegar. It also has no smell, which is certainly not the case for the vinegar. The US Postal Service delivers citric acid to my door, which means it is much easier to acquire. I mainly use citric acid, but there are times when vinegar (because it does not need to be mixed with anything to use) is the liquid for the job. Therefore, I keep both in the studio. Cider vinegar works in a pinch; however, it should only be used in recipes where a little extra golden color won't negatively affect the outcome.

Pint jars and lids at the ready provide a quick and easy way to save unused mixed dye for another day. They also do double duty as mixing vessels for dye methods that require more separate colors than the number of measuring cups in your studio.

Long-handled spoons and a **potato masher** come in handy for stirring, mashing down, and redistributing pieces of wool.

I'll admit these next three aren't very glamorous. Still, I won't leave home without one or two cheap **buckets**, a spray bottle of **bleach**, and a good **stainless steel cleaner**.

Several dye techniques work better if the wool is pre-soaked in a tub of water laced with some sort of **wetting agent**. While clear Synthrapol is my presoak liquid of choice, Dawn or Jet Dry can substitute in a pinch. If you are using those substitutes, please remember that they come colored and will need to be thoroughly mixed in the soaking bath before any wool is added.

Dye Kitchen Tools and Setup

7. Storage

You can have all the right equipment in the world, but if it is not easily accessible, usage becomes a problem. More than that, finding it becomes a problem! Consequently, I consider storage units to be an essential part of a good workspace. Whatever you choose, they should be strong, flexible as to arrangement, visually easy to use, and impervious to heat and moisture.

This plastic-coated wire shelf hangs directly above the draining board of my stainless sink. Once measuring cups, mixing spoons, and dye spoons are washed, they sit or hang on the wire rack to drip dry over the sink.

Every bit of space in the studio should be utilized for effective storage. My stainless steel tables have adjustable bottom shelves. After taking the wheels off this black mechanic's tool chest, I was able to slide it into the available space. I store basic tools (it's amazing how often I need a hammer and a screwdriver in the dye lab) and power cords in this unit. Lesser tables would not be able to handle the extreme weight of this tool chest.

As you can probably tell, I like to use commercial restaurant equipment in my studio. Made to thrive in hot, steamy environments, this sort of equipment is perfect for the home dyer. Shelving units like this are a natural choice for dye pots and pans because they were designed to hold pots and pans. I don't even mind putting slightly dripping pots and pans on them because the open shelves don't easily rust or allow moisture to pool, and they let any drips pass through to my concrete floor. By easily reconfiguring the placement of the shelves, dedicated spaces for certain pots can be created. Just like tools on a pegboard, most of my pots only have one place they can fit, which also has the benefit of making it easier for me to remember where to find them.

Coated wire shelving is lightweight and sight-friendly in addition to being rust resistant. Consequently, these stackable Elfa units are perfect for the actual "dye powder" section of the studio.

By taking jars of dye with me on my search for the perfect storage solution, I was able to guarantee the construction of a shelving unit that was configured to suit my special needs before I bought it. The bottom shelf of my stainless table was easily adjusted to hold this double unit. All my Pro Chem dyes are easily stored in numerical order.

The much smaller packets of Cushing Dyes, arranged in alphabetical order, get their own shallow storage drawer. An additional shallow drawer holds recipe books and other top-secret information.

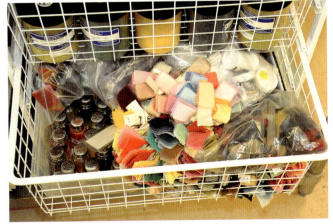

Majic Carpet dyes, dye samples, salt shakers, and other similar dye paraphernalia get stored away in another easily accessible drawer.

Dye Kitchen Tools and Setup

PREPPING FIBER BEFORE YOU DYE

chapter 2

▲▲▲
A little fiber prep work will help eliminate the guesswork of dyeing.
▲▲▲

Home dyers are delighted to find that they can dye a variety of fibers—everything from wool and nylon fabric to wool yarn and fleece.

Wool Fabric

Regardless of whether your wool fabric comes off the bolt or out of your stash, it will need some sort of prepping before it can be dyed. Practically speaking, pieces need to be cut to an easily managed size. Additionally, you have to know how much wool fabric is being dyed in order to determine the amount of dry dye you need. When a standard method of measurement is employed on new wool, before it is dyed, it is much easier to determine both wool and dye amounts that you might need for either dyeing or hooking.

What is one yard? By measuring out yardage with the selvedge as a baseline, a 36-inch length when snipped and ripped across the entire width of the bolt will equal one yard of wool. That is how the manufacturer prices wool and the buyer purchases it. Trying to sort wool out after it is dyed is a real problem. Yes, all wool shrinks (about 10 percent) when dyed—it just doesn't always shrink the same amount. Additionally, bolts of fabric come in various widths due to both manufacturer choice and the way that different weave structures behave after coming off the loom. Since everyone buys new wool based on yard increments cut on the selvedge edge, it is best to use that measurement as a baseline. I even recommend that you take your prepping a little further so that you can easily identify $1/2$, $1/4$, $1/8$, and $1/16$ yard pieces.

I use two different methods to prep my wool fabric: a short cut or a long cut.

TIP — ACCURATE LINES

Using fabric store cutting tables for inspiration, I marked all my 6-foot plastic worktables at 18-inch intervals. It is easy to make accurate measuring lines using a T-square and a permanent marker. By drawing lines 18 inches apart over the surfaces of my tables, I now have plenty of space to unwrap and then snip the wool at whichever length is desired.

Short Cut

A short cut produces pieces that are 18 inches long at the selvedge, before dyeing, and incrementally marked at $1/4$-, $1/8$-, and $1/16$-yard sections. This prep method is particularly good for those who like to end up with cut strips that are not overly long (about $16 1/2$ inches when dyed). Short cuts are also ideal for wool pieces needed to make marbleized wool.

Step 1 (right): After unrolling a few turns of wool, position the torn edge at the first mark, with the selvedge running down past the second mark. Use a pair of sharp scissors to snip a notch at the 18-inch mark. Once snipped, the wool can easily be torn across the width of the bolt. Wool should always be snipped and then torn so that it will tear straight with the weft of the fabric. Once this tear is completed, the end result will be a full $1/2$ yard of wool the width of the bolt (58 inches) and 18 inches long.

Step 2: After tearing is completed, fold the fabric in half so the selvedge edges (left) are together. Thus folded, the resultant piece is approximately 18 by 29 inches.

At the fold, use a sharp pair of scissors to snip a notch. This new snip allows you to create two $1/4$-yard pieces out of the original $1/2$ yard. While it could be torn at this moment, a bit more folding and notching will produce even more helpful markers.

A Bit about Selvedges

Since selvedges are much thicker than the wool fabric, they should be removed before the piece is cut up into hooking strips. Think of the selvedge as "wool rind" or excess wool fat that needs to be trimmed. If the removal is not taken into account when you fold the wool, the pieces with selvedge will get short-changed, making those pieces a bit smaller than the full pieces without selvedge. Measuring up to the end of the selvedge anticipates this event and takes the selvedge out of the equation.

Why not just remove the selvedges before folding? You can do that if you wish. However, I like to leave the selvedges on until the dyed pieces are ready to head to their final destination. If the selvedge is still on the wool, there is no question about selvedge direction. It is a good marker until it is no longer needed.

Step 3: After making that first snip at the initial fold on the right side, grasp that snipped corner and fold it over to the selvedge side on the left. This shot shows the original ½-yard piece folded so that that the piece is now four layers thick. Notice that the first fold is not placed even with the edge of the two selvedges. The edge of the original fold has been brought to rest at the spot where the fabric ends and the selvedge begins.

After carefully folding the wool so the selvedge is excluded on the left, notch at the fold through both layers on the right.

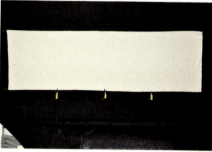

At this point, if you were to open up the ½-yard (18-inch) piece, we could easily see that it has three visible notches evenly spaced to create four ⅛-yard pieces. If torn at the notches, the interior pieces would make a perfect ⅛ yard. The pieces on each outside edge, however, are ⅛ yard plus a selvedge.

Step 4: While four markers are good, more folds and notches are even better. To make ¹⁄₁₆-yard notches, fold those top two layers (the ones just touching the selvedge) back to the center fold and notch the new fold on the left. Those new notched pieces each measure ¹⁄₁₆ yard.

Step 5: Finalize the procedure by folding over the edges with the selvedge. Because the selvedge will be eventually torn off, remember to position the selvedge so that it sticks over the cut marker at about the place (½ inch) where it will be torn. One little snip at the fold marks the final ¹⁄₁₆-yard piece. Any of these cuts can work very well for most applications.

Long Cut

The short 18-inch cut just discussed produces a length of about $16\frac{1}{2}$ inches of useable wool after dyeing. That size is similar to what rug hookers have been relying on for many decades. In fact, some of my earliest instruction in rug hooking told me that wool strips should never be longer than that because they would be too hard to run through a cutter.

While the width of a piece may affect the way wool goes through a cutter (wide pieces want to hang off the left edge), length does not. More and more, I prefer longer cuts of wool so that I can hook longer rows without having to add in new pieces. Longer strips also mean fewer tails. Consequently, for many of the dye methods in this book, I recommend the long cut method—36-inch cuts at the selvedge—as it provides more options to the fiber artist.

When dyed, a 36-inch piece will shrink down to about $32\frac{1}{4}$ inches, or roughly twice as long as the short cut. Additionally, even when prepped and dyed "long," finished wool can always be turned into the shorter version with a fold and a snip at the center. One other benefit to the long cut is that you can save time by only having to prep one edge per yard.

Step 1: Measuring from the torn edge of bolt wool, make a snip on the selvedge at the 36-inch mark. Tear the wool across the entire width of the bolt to produce a single piece that is 1 yard long.

Step 2: Follow all the folding and snipping steps described in the short cut method. As the piece of fabric being worked is twice as long as before, each snip and tear will produce a piece of wool that is twice as big as the short cut. For example, a piece torn at the short $\frac{1}{16}$ yard will be $\frac{1}{8}$ yard. A piece torn at the short $\frac{1}{8}$-yard snip will be $\frac{1}{4}$ yard. And so on.

Jumbo Long Cuts

If your particular dye technique can handle it, why not dye pieces that will produce really long jumbo strips?

Verson 1: If selvedge direction makes no difference to you, instead of measuring at 18 inches or 36 inches along the selvedge, consider making your initial cut at just 9 inches. **Result:** A 9-inch piece, measured at the selvedge and torn the width of the bolt, makes a perfect one-quarter yard of fabric that will be about 53 inches long when dyed. **Benefit:** That is a great length for borders, background, fabric needle punch, and other applications for which you should ideally hook as long as possible before adding in a new piece.

Version 2: Why limit yourself to pieces that are just one yard long? It is just as easy to cut at 54 inches ($1\frac{1}{2}$ yards) or 72 inches (2 yards). You can still fold and notch at the top as previously described. **Benefit:** On a 72-inch-long piece, a short $\frac{1}{8}$-yard mark will produce a piece that is $\frac{1}{2}$ yard overall. It might be perfect for a special dip dye.

Prepping Wool by Weight

Rug hookers often use irregular recycled wool from garments as well as odd-sized leftover pieces from other projects, so there are many instances when it is impossible to use a yardstick to determine wool amounts. In those cases, bundles of wool can be weighed to determine their amount. Normal hooking wool is considered "flannel" weight and weighs roughly $\frac{3}{4}$ pound (12 ounces) per yard. With that designation, it is safe to figure that $1\frac{1}{2}$ pounds of wool would equal about 2 yards of wool. On the other hand, 6 ounces would be about $\frac{1}{2}$ yard of wool.

Prepping Wool by Sight

While it may not be too precise, a known piece of wool can be used as a template for measuring odd pieces of wool. All you have to do is lay a $\frac{1}{4}$-yard piece of dyed wool on a table, then start laying the odd pieces down in mosaic fashion until the template is covered. Don't have a known piece of wool? Make your own template. A $16\frac{1}{2}$-inch by $26\frac{1}{2}$-inch rectangular piece of paper is roughly the size of a standard $\frac{1}{4}$ yard of dyed, felted wool or 18 inches by 29 inches of undyed, unshrunk wool.

Wool Prep Tips to Remember

Fabric Size Varies from Bolt to Bolt

Even if you are using brand new wool, you will still find variation from manufacturer to manufacturer: one 36-inch selvedge-cut piece of wool can be a bit wider or narrower than another 36-inch selvedge piece from a different bolt. During a quick check of the width of the bolts on my shelf, I found several different widths ranging from 57 inches to 62 inches wide. Consequently, a 36-inch-long piece of wool that is 2 inches wider than another 36-inch-long piece of wool is going to end up dyeing slightly lighter because it has more wool to soak up the color than the narrower piece.

So, if you are really concerned about producing a certain color and value, precisely measure each piece of wool off the same bolt and keep track of the exact measurements of dry dye being used. If you are using odds and ends in various shapes and sizes, weigh your dry pieces until you get a stack that is $\frac{3}{4}$ pound, the approximate weight of 1 yard of flannel-weight wool.

Shrinkage

Remember that all wool shrinks when it goes through the dyeing, rinsing, and drying process. Although the actual amount varies from piece to piece, plan on a loss of about 10 percent in length and about 3 percent in width. Consequently, a predyed piece that measured 18 inches will probably end up being about 16¼ inches long when dyed. Take this into consideration if you need the dye process to produce fabric in a specific length.

A dip-dyed piece for a scroll would be such an application. If you are hooking, for example, a scroll with a "line" that is 10 inches long, and you are also allowing that the loops call for an additional increase in length (four times), you will need a 40-inch-long dyed strip. To get a piece that long, however, you will need to start out with a length that is at least 10 percent longer to allow for shrinkage—or about 44 or 45 inches long. Cut the wool at whatever length will allow you to achieve your need.

Does Selvedge Direction Matter?

In the wool fabric measuring procedures described, I use notches at intervals to both measure amounts and indicate the selvedge direction. In the resultant pieces, even after the selvedge has been removed, the notches always mirror the original selvedge. If you consistently measure and notch wool in this way, you will always know which way the selvedge runs.

Why does this matter? Traditionally, rug hookers have felt that wool should be cut with the direction of the selvedge. I simply have not found most of the reasons given to be legitimate, with one possible exception: **if you are hooking with #3 or #4 cuts**, cutting with the selvedge may help the narrow strips hold together a tad bit better. Since strip integrity is a problem for those narrow cuts, I always notch and cut that wool with the selvedge. I am really not sure it helps, but I like to think that it does. However, **if you know the wool is intended for wider cuts (#5 to #12)**, it does not matter which straight direction the strips are cut in as long as it is with the warp or weft—not diagonal!

Wool Yarn

Even though it comes in a different shape than its woven sister, wool yarn is still wool fiber that is willing to soak up whatever it can in the right dye bath. However, where fabric is fairly easy to manage, wool yarn can turn into a big rat's nest if you don't properly prep it before dyeing.

Since most skeins weigh 3.5 or 4 ounces, about the same amount as ⅓ yard of wool fabric, each skein can be dyed with the same amount of dye that you would use to dye that amount of fabric. You can also substitute that much yarn in place of equal fabric in any dye recipe.

The only problem with that instruction is that both my torn wool technique and dry measure dye spoons split up

Before doing anything to a skein of wool yarn, take note of its weight and structure. These three skeins represent the main types of wool yarn in this book: bulky weight rug yarn, medium weight commercial yarn, and whipping yarn. Although all three skeins weigh the same amount, 4 ounces, they are produced in very different ways for very different uses. The top skein is commercial Halcyon Yarn Rug Wool specifically made to punch or hook rugs. Because of its bulky girth, it measures only about 65 yards. The middle skein is also commercial Halcyon Rug Wool (Deco Variety) but is spun in such a way that it is much thinner and measures about 115 yards in length. It is produced for rug hooking, finer needle punch, and weaving projects. The bottom skein is privately produced by Maple Terrace Farm in British Columbia, Canada. Yardage from this skein is approximately 190 yards and it is perfect for whipping the edges of my rugs. Despite their varying lengths, each skein weighs the same as ⅓ yard of wool fabric.

better in halves, quarters, and eighths, not thirds. To compensate for that inequity, I recommend one of these approaches:

1. Dye three 4-ounce skeins at one time (total weight is equal to 1 yard) and use dry measurements as you would for any technique using one yard of wool.

2. Should you only want to dye one 4-ounce skein, while being extremely accurate with a specific formula, measure out enough dry dye for one yard (12 ounces) of wool. Mix the dye with 1 cup of boiling water. Pour out $1/3$ cup of the mixed dye solution, and use it to dye the single 4-ounce skein of yarn. Reserve the excess mixed dye for another project

3. My favorite way to compensate, however, is this: Treat each 4-ounce skein as though it were equal to $1/4$ yard of fabric, but be a little generous with the dry dye measurement. For example, if I am substituting a 4-ounce skein of yarn for $1/4$ yard of fabric in a batch designed for 1 yard of fabric, then I'll think of the $3/4$ yard of fabric and one skein as 1 heavy yard of wool. If my dye recipe calls for $1/2$ tsp. of dye for 1 yard of wool, I'll measure out a *rounded or heaping* $1/2$ tsp. of dye instead of a precise $1/2$ tsp. Since 4 ounces of yarn weighs a little more than $1/4$ yard of fabric, I dye the batch with a little bigger amount of the dye recipe I am using. It is just that simple.

Prepping an Entire Skein

A skein of twisted yarn needs to be released from its twist in order for the dye to freely penetrate into the wool.

Manufacturers usually secure the loose strands at one spot before packaging or twisting. Even if you are dyeing the entire skein as it comes out of the twist, it is always a good idea to secure it in at least one or two other spots so that the yarn can't come undone or get tangled. Because cooking, rinsing, and wringing all jostle the yarn a great deal, make sure you take the time to ensure that it will stay organized during the process.

Use a 10-inch piece of natural (undyed) "holding yarn" for new cross ties to stabilize the yarn. (I've used red yarn for demonstration purposes, but never use yarn that can bleed a different color than you want.) Divide a section of the skein into two or three clusters. Go around the first section with the holding yarn, then cross the two ends of the holding yarn so that the first section is loosely contained. Proceed over a second section and contain it with a new cross. Repeat a time or two in order to contain the wool. Make a final knotted tie so that the holding yarn cannot come undone. Small skeins may need just two crosses; big skeins may need three or four.

When adding the holding ties, keep them fairly loose so that the wool is not restricted at these spots. If tied too tightly, the yarn can't accept the color, as seen in the white spots on this skein.

Prepping a Smaller Amount of Yarn

Since I mainly use yarn to whip my hooked rugs, I rarely want to dye entire skeins. Here is a practical way to break down a skein into smaller amounts. A little specialized equipment can provide an extra hand or two.

A traditional swift (right) is perfect for holding yarn. This beautiful, classic, cherry wood swift opens up like an umbrella, holding the yarn in an organized fashion until the artist is ready for it. The mechanism revolves as the yarn is pulled and measured. The other article being used in this photo (left) is an extremely ugly, bowed piece of 2-by-4 lumber that came off a scrap pile! Four pegs are positioned in the board, two at each end, so that one complete trip around the four pegs measures a perfect 2 yards (72 inches). I glued three of the four pegs in their holes while the fourth is loose for easy removal.

All you have to do to get started with this system is tie a loop at the end of the yarn and then slip it over any one of the pegs on the 2-by-4. Taking care not to stretch the yarn too much, wrap the yarn around the entire circuit of pegs. It is a simple matter to keep track of the yardage as every complete trip adds another 2 yards to the total. Take note of the fact that a 10-inch piece of yarn rests underneath the first layer of measured wool. There is an identical piece under the measured yarn at the other end.

After making 10 complete trips around the pegs, the extra pieces of yarn at each end are crossed over the measured wool. They will stay in that position until 10 more trips around the pegs are made. At the 20th pass, the ends of the short yarn will make yet another cross, repeating this with every 10 passes until the desired amount is measured out. Since the short wool pieces are crossed every 10 (20 yard) passes, it is very easy to tell exactly how much yarn has been measured. When you are finished with the last trip, make sure to leave an extra 12 inches before you cut the yarn.

Once the last trip has been made, the shorter cross pieces can be tied into a bow or knot to secure the yarn. Take care not to pull that final tie so tight as to restrict the wool. It is a good idea to do this in a two-step process: make the first tie to secure the wool, then fold the extra length of tail back over the cross tie and tie it a second time to fix the tail in place. By finishing in this way, you can always find the beginning of the yarn.

When removed from the pegs, the secured sections of the wool ought to look like this.

Once the measuring is done, retwist the wool until it is needed. Yarn tends to be very mischievous and, without careful supervision, will get into trouble. Keeping several small twists like this prepped and ready to go for those impulse dyeing sessions makes it really easy to always have coordinated whipping wool on hand for all your special projects. Additionally, such a small amount of wool hardly affects the color value of most dye pots.

Soaking Fiber Before Dyeing

Most dye techniques, particularly those over natural or white fiber, respond best to wool that has been properly soaked in warm water with some type of wetting agent. This combination of hot water and additive opens up the fibers in the wool so that they will be receptive to the color in the dye bath. Receptive fiber will welcome color to its very core. In fact, when color does not go into the fiber, you can see a white core when the fabric is cut. In other words, dye can't get inside the fiber unless the door is open. Commercial agents like Synthrapol help open the door. However, Jet Dry and even Dawn dishwashing liquid will work in a pinch. While the easiest place to soak several yards of wool is in the well of a sink, buckets, tubs, and big pots work just fine.

Rules for a Basic Soak

Rule 1: While filling your container of choice with hot water, add the Synthrapol—a scant teaspoon per gallon, according to the manufacturer's instructions. If using Dawn instead, swish it around in the water very well before adding any fiber as a straight shot of the blue detergent can stain the fabric or wool.

Rule 2: Add the fiber after most of the hot water has been placed in the holding container. If you are adding several pieces of fabric, add them one at a time so layers of wool don't form a pack. Use your hand to stir the fabric well; make sure all the fiber comes in contact with the water. Once the wool has been stirred, push it under the water.

Rule 3: Soak the fiber long enough in the right solution. Of course, this rule begs the question: how long is enough? When I have a dye session scheduled, I soak my wool overnight so it is ready for me first thing in the morning when I hit the studio. However, an effective soak is a combination of time, heat, and wetting agent. In fact, if I had to choose between length of soak time and warmth of soak water, I would choose more heat and less time. In other words, I find a 2-hour Synthrapol soak in controlled (maintained) hot water to be just as effective as an all-night soak in cool water. The first thing I do on dyeing day is boil up a pot or two of water that can raise the temperature of my soaking wool.

Rule 4: When soaking colored wool, sort and soak by color. If your dye session includes the overdyeing of yellow, red, blue, and some natural, don't soak all those colors together. If you do, you may find that some have bled out during the soak, thereby affecting most of the colored wool before it ever hits the dye pot. You run the same risk when soaking generic pieces of grey and tan tweed in the same soaking pot with natural. Even a cold water soak with those pieces will quickly produce a muddy liquid. So if you want to soak colors, soak them separately. (Remember, I told you to get some cheap buckets.)

However, for many methods I use, soaking is not necessary at all. After all, yellow wool does not have a white core. When I overdye yellow fabric with green dye, I want to produce green wool with yellow highlights—that is the whole idea. Should I get a little bit of yellow core in that process, it is just fine. I only soak colored wool when I want to affect the host wool down to its very core. I also soak light tweeds as they could easily end up with light cores, but I soak them in their own pot.

NOTE Instructions on prepping mohair, fleece, and roving are given in batch 14.

How Much Wool Do I Need to Whip a Rug?

The answer, of course, depends on the size of the rug, the method you use to whip, and the weight of yarn you choose. For a simple whipped edge, I find that a 72-inch length of yarn, doubled in the needle to sew two strands of 36 inches, will cover about 6 to 7 inches of whipped edge. If you take the time to do the math on regular weight whipping yarn, most 4-ounce skeins will produce enough dyed wool to whip three 5-foot by 3-foot hooked rugs. Therefore, instead of dyeing entire skeins of wool that will produce far more whipping yarn than needed for a standard project, break down the big skeins into more reasonable amounts as described in the section Prepping a Smaller Amount of Yarn.

Using the 2-by-4 method mentioned, I make a smaller skein with about 33 two-yard wraps. Even with shrinkage after dyeing, this smaller skein will whip a 3-foot by 5-foot rug. Since most rugs are much smaller than that, 33 revolutions will guarantee plenty of extra whipping wool for the projects that most people do. I make these smaller skeins up in advance so one is always ready should I have the impulse to dye wool for a rug. If you have a larger hooked project, two prepped skeins, instead of one, can be thrown into the dye pot.

DYEING WITH COMMERCIAL ACID DYES

chapter 3

Commercial Acid Dye Q&A

Before using acid dyes, let's answer some common questions and establish some ground rules.

> ▲▲▲
> Whether used alone or mixed with other colors, acid dyes provide a veritable rainbow for the home dyer.
> ▼▼▼

What is an acid dye?

Just the term "acid dye" makes some people incredibly nervous! *You use acid dyes? Are you crazy? Aren't you afraid you will burn a hole in the wool or maybe even your pot? What if you get some on you?* While I rather like cultivating the image of an edgy mad scientist/fiber artist with test tubes and beakers of smoky liquids doing my thing while sinister organ music plays in the background, it's really not all that exciting.

Commercial acid dyes are made specifically for protein fibers like wool, mohair, and nylon. They get their "acid" designation because they need to have acid applied during the dye process so that the color will make a molecular bond with the fiber. In other words, the dyer adds safe, natural acids to the commercial dyes during the process; the commercial dye does not come as a toxic substance.

The traditional acid of choice has long been clear vinegar (acetic acid), which people have in their kitchen cupboards. Colored vinegar would also work, although it may affect some of the colors being dyed.

While I am not opposed to using clear vinegar, I much prefer citric acid crystals. Since the crystals have a 56 percent acidity rate compared to a 5 percent acidity rate for vinegar, it takes more vinegar ($1/2$ to $3/4$ cup) than citric acid crystals (1 Tbsp.) to set 1 yard of wool. By using the citric acid crystals, I save space and money and avoid the strong smell of vinegar in the studio.

If acid dyes are so safe, then why are masks and gloves recommended?

Masks: Any time you come into contact with powder of any kind, you can have a reaction to it. It makes no difference if the airborne powder is baby powder, wheat flour, cornstarch, or dry dye; it can be inhaled into your lungs and cause irritation. (In the early stages of fatherhood, I was rendered inactive for several hours due to the use of way too much baby powder.) As some people are particularly sensitive to airborne powder, a simple mask provides protection. For this reason, dry dye manufacturers recommend that a mask be worn when airborne dye powder could be inhaled. Additionally, some people breathe powder for years with no ill effects then suddenly develop a reaction. Masks only block airborne powder; they don't protect from noxious fumes. But that's fine because the dye process produces no noxious fumes.

Gloves: The manufacturers recommend that you wear gloves so that you can keep your hands clean! Unless you have an open wound, mixed dye is not absorbed through the skin.

My Top 20 Colors

I'm asked one question all the time: "What colors of dye should I buy?" The short answer is this: "Buy the colors that appeal to you." However, as you will find when dyeing the various projects in this book, many of our dye colors end up producing wool that does not look like the manufacturer's swatch. Those swatches have hidden qualities that don't come out unless properly coaxed. Consequently, you can't always read a color by its swatch cover. Therefore, should the government draft me as the wool dyer for a colonization project on a distant planet with the instructions that I could only take 20 Pro Chem Acid Dyes with me, these are the ones I would take:

- 122 Mustard
- 123 Toffee
- 135 Yellow
- 338 Magenta
- 351 Bright Red
- 407 Sky Blue
- 409 Brilliant Blue
- 411 Periwinkle
- 506 Tan
- 508 Mahogany
- 561 Clay
- 672 Jet Black
- 707 Avocado
- 709 Herb Green
- 713 Olive Drab
- 733 Ivy
- 808 Raspberry
- 813 Deep Purple
- 827 Grape Juice
- 845 Acid Lilac

Personal note to the following colors:

- 120 Golden Pear
- 121 Maple Sugar
- 130 Caramel
- 199c Golden Yellow
- 339 Lobster Bisque
- 478 Turquoise
- 501 MochaChino
- 503 Brown
- 714 Mallard
- 819 Purple
- 822 Plum
- 826 Deep Orchid

You know I love you and would never have excluded you from that silly Top 20 limited list except that they forced me to do so. Still, we must be together, and I will find a way to smuggle you on board. I can't contemplate life without you. GRS

Commercial acid dyes are made specifically for protein fibers like wool, mohair, and nylon. They get their "acid" designation because they need to have acid applied during the dye process so that the color will make a molecular bond with the fiber. In other words, the dyer adds safe, natural acids to the commercial dyes during the process; the commercial dye does not come as a toxic substance.

How does the process work?

Six things must come together for the success of each dye batch in this book. Unless otherwise instructed, you should always follow these five directives:

1. Presoak the fiber in a combination of water and a wetting agent like Synthrapol.

2. Mix each dye recipe in boiling water, taking care to stir the mixture until all dry dye is completely incorporated.

3. Always cook the fiber at 212°F or a little hotter. When instructions are given using phrases such as "bring the kettle to a boil," "simmer the fiber," or "bake in the oven," your goal is to cook the wool during the entire time at a minimum of 212°F. You do not need to carry around a thermometer to find this temperature. Heat your pots and pans until the water boils and bubbles and then keep it bubbling during the entire process. If there aren't some bubbles, then it isn't hot enough. If you are using an oven, set the temperature a little higher (275°F–300°F) as oven dye techniques usually have thicker stacks of fiber and need a little extra heat to reach an internal temperature of 212°F.

4. Add the acid—either citric acid or white vinegar—at the time indicated in the instructions for the specific method you are using. It takes about 1 Tbsp. of citric acid or 2/3 cup of vinegar to set a yard of wool. If that doesn't seem to be enough in any dyeing session, you can add a little more.

5. Cook each batch for 1 hour. It matters not when the water clears or what you think has or has not happened; if you want to make wool that has been properly penetrated by dye, as well as properly set, cook the fiber for 1 hour at 212°F.

6. Let the dyed wool cool down in the pot.

How much dye will I need?

Unless you have a set recipe, it is always a bit of a challenge to know how much dry dye to mix for any given pile of wool. My general rule of thumb, for a medium value background, is to use about 1/2 tsp. of dye to 1 yard of fabric—a little less to get lighter wool and a little more to get darker wool. If dyeing 1/2 yard of wool, the dye amount would drop down to 1/4 tsp. of dye: 1/4 yard would take 1/8 tsp., and so on. If using new, off-bolt wool, it is relatively easy to get precise amounts of wool.

What needs to be done when a dye session is over?

Cool Down: Certain colors, particularly turquoise and other blues, benefit from some cool-down time in the pot. While it is not necessary to wait until the water is cold, even a short wait will help these colors finish their bonding process with the wool. Cooling is to wool coloration what aging is to cheese—it ripens it.

Cold Water Rinse #1: I always rinse my dyed wool in cold water. Although I recommend that you allow your wool to cool down in the pot before this first rinse, I am always a bit taken aback when I read information about how you can't rinse hot or warm wool with cold water because it will shock the wool. I do it all the time with no adverse effects.

Rinse #2: After the initial rinse and hand wring to remove excess moisture, my wool goes in a second tub of clear water where it is submersed and rinsed again.

Final Wringing: On leisurely dyeing days, the second rinse tub is a stainless steel portable sink equipped with a hand wringer. On hectic days, the wool is taken to the washing machine and run through just the spin cycle to remove the excess water. I never rinse my wool in a washing machine. While wool can take extremes of heat, cold, wringing, and other abuse, I find that even minimal agitation in any washing machine cycle tends to cause more felting than I want.

Drying: On leisurely days, the wool goes on the clothesline. This is my preference if the sun is not beating down with a scorching heat. When the sun is brutally hot, I hang the wool on my sheltered patio. On hectic days, after coming out of the spin cycle, the wool goes in the dryer along with a couple of thick bath towels. I keep an eye on the length of the drying cycle, leaving the wool in only long enough to accomplish the task.

I prefer citric acid crystals to vinegar. It takes far less citric acid crystals than vinegar to set 1 yard of wool. By using the citric acid crystals, I save space and money and avoid the strong smell of vinegar in the studio.

PART TWO: DYEING IN BATCHES

Do You Want To Use Commercial Dyes?

If you are ready, willing, and able to purchase and use commercial dyes, the first 15 batches in this section are just for you. Designed in such a way as to help you progress in your understanding and expertise, each batch, and its multiple variations, can be followed as described or adapted to suit your own needs.

Do You Want To Dye Without Dye?

Odd as that question may seem, batches 16 through 19 are designed for the home dyer who cannot or does not want to buy, store, or use commercial dyes. These four batches give a tremendous number of options that will allow you to either dye new wool or repurpose and recycle found wool of all kinds.

DYEING WITH COMMERCIAL ACID DYE

batch 1

Solid Color with No Mottling

▲▲▲
To dye wool in one even color with no mottling highs or lows, think "more": More water, more space, more stirring, more time before acid.
▲▲▲

Ways to Use Solid Colors

▲ Projects that demand a solid, even color

▲ Back side of a pillow project

▲ Solid color backgrounds for appliqué and hooking projects

▲ Quilt binding

▲ Solid color yarn

RESULT: PC #407 SKY BLUE OVER NATURAL WOOL

¼ tsp. PC #407 Sky Blue over ½ yard presoaked natural wool fabric

This first batch is ideal for those who like solid color wool fabric or yarn with little or no variation. Extra water and extra stirring in an extra big space allow the wool to spread out so that it can evenly soak up the dye. The principle is not unlike the criterion someone might use to select a good place to take a bubble bath. Where would you be more apt to stretch out and soak up all those bubbles? A big claw-foot bathtub, for example, would be a much better choice than a small kitchen sink. The same is true for dyeing evenly colored wool. For this particular example, a 2½-gallon pot will provide plenty of relaxed soaking space for ½ yard of wool.

26 Prepared to Dye

Decorative Stitches Sampler, *15" x 15", #4-cut solid-colored dyed wool on monk's cloth. Hooked by Joyce Fortney, Homasassa, Florida, 2000.*

In order for the fields of color in the precise stitches of this design to be sharp and well defined, each strip of wool needed to be constant, without highs and lows of value.

Step 1: Fill a clean 2½-gallon pot with fresh water until it is approximately half to two-thirds full. Heat until the water comes to a rolling boil.

Step 2: Carefully measure the amount of dry dye you will need. For this particular medium value bath, ¼ tsp. PC #407 Sky Blue was used over ½ yard presoaked natural wool. After filling the spoon with dry dye, the most precise way of leveling off the excess dye is to scrape a toothpick, or some other similar straight edge, across the top of the spoon. (Since I am not usually worried about that level of precise control, I gently tap the dye spoon against the side of the dye container.) Once the spoon content is leveled to your satisfaction, turn the measuring spoon upside down into a clean measuring cup. Rap it against the side of the cup to dislodge all the dye. When emptied, remove the dye spoon.

Step 3: Once the dye comes out of the dye spoon, I immediately stick the spoon in a jar of coarse kosher salt and swish it around. The dry salt acts like a dye sandblaster, cleaning the spoon so it is ready to go for the next batch.

Step 4: Add 1 cup of hot water to the measuring cup with the dye. Use a generic tablespoon to stir. The stirring step is important: bits of dye can hide in the corners of the measuring cup, evading incorporation unless the mixture is thoroughly stirred.

Step 5: Since mixed dye can react to the water in a dye pot, turn off the heat source under a boiling pot before adding dye. Carefully pour the mixed dye into the pot.

Step 6: Check the measuring cup for residual dye. If there is any, keep stirring until everything is incorporated. Finish the mixing process by giving the cup a bob and rinse in the dye pot water. Stir the big pot with a long-handled spoon or tongs. Everything needs to be mixed well in order to have one consistent color. Turn on the heat and bring the dye bath to a boil.

Step 7: Remove ½ yard wool (two ¼-yard pieces) from the soaking bath, and wring out the excess water.

Step 8: When the dye bath has come to a good boil, it is ready. Although a hard boil temperature would be too much for the entire cooking process of this batch, remember that the much colder wool (even if it is hot to the touch) will immediately bring down the temperature of the pot. Cooler wool helps self-adjust the pot, still keeping the dye bath hot enough to begin its work. I prefer this method of toning down hot wool to the right

> **Must I Cover the Dye Pot?**
>
> The short answer is no. After all, some of my pots don't even have lids, and I use them all the time. Additionally, some of my gas burners put out more heat than others. In that situation, a lid almost makes the pot too hot to handle. The only way I can keep things regulated is by leaving off the lid. On the other hand, if I'm using electric hot plates and a host of other appliances where getting enough heat is a problem, a lid—even a cookie sheet over a pot—will improve that situation. When I can, I like to use lids, and I buy pots that come with them because I want the option of using a lid—or not. Finally, with all the steam and condensation taking place in a studio when six burners are going at once, lids bring a bit of order to the atmosphere.

temperature. If you add wool that stops a boil, then everything just sits in the pot while it tries to catch up the heat.

Step 9: Pick up each piece of wool (two pieces in this case) at its middle point so that it can spread out as it hangs loosely.

28   Prepared to Dye

Step 10: The goal is to drop the "open" fabric into the dye bath in as quick and smooth a fashion as possible; it should not be folded or twisted. Remember, this wool needs to spread out so it can evenly soak up the dye.

Step 11: As soon as the wool goes in, begin stirring the pot so that every bit of the fabric is kept on the move, making continual contact with the dye bath. Keep the wool from resting or forming pockets or folds until the fabric has time to soak up the color. After adding the wool, if the water is still at a hard boil, turn down the heat so that it is simmering. In other words, you want to see some bubbling going on but not a hard, vigorous, rolling boil.

Step 12: Cook and stir until the wool has accepted most of the dye. This will be fairly obvious, as the dye bath will lose most of its blue color. You can easily check the progress of this process by using a measuring cup to scoop up a sample for a quick assessment.

Step 13: Once the bath water is basically clear, add 1 scant Tbsp. of citric acid or 1/2 cup or more of clear vinegar, continuing to stir for the next couple of minutes. Cover the pot with a lid and cook at a simmer for 1 hour. Stir the wool every few minutes. Because the temperature in a covered pot will increase, adjust the heat as necessary to keep the bath at that simmering point. There is nothing magic about using a lid other than the fact that it helps keep everything in the pot at the right temperature to accept the dye. A lid also condenses the steam, redirecting water back into the dye pot. Even with a lid—and certainly without one—check every so often to make sure the pot has more than enough water to keep the fiber from scorching. You can add more clear water at any time.

Step 14: If you add clear water at any time in the dye process, be sure to add boiling water so as not to slow down the hour-long dyeing process. If you are using a stove with extra burners, keep some water boiling in a pot just for that purpose.

At the end of the hour of cook time, all the dye should have gone into the wool, leaving a clear bath of water.

Yarn? You Bet!

The solid color technique described here works just as well for wool yarn as it does for wool fabric. In this case, 6 ounces of yarn (usually 1 1/2 skeins) would equal the same amount of wool as found in 1/2 yard of woven fabric, requiring 1/4 tsp. dye to get the same basic result. If splitting skeins is a problem, double the dry dye to 1/2 tsp. and use it over three 4-ounce skeins. For rug hookers who would like just enough yarn to whip a finished rug, which would be far less than 6 ounces, toss in a small amount of yarn along with the initial pieces of wool fabric.

Solid Color with No Mottling   29

DYEING WITH COMMERCIAL ACID DYE

batch 2

Solid Color with Mottling

▲▲▲

For a mottled or splotchy dye effect, think "less": less water, less stirring, less wait before acid.

▲▲▲

Ways to Use Mottled Wool

- Good for most rug hooking applications
- Creates yarn with high and low values of the same color
- Good for appliqué and penny rug projects
- Desirable for those who like their wool to have some variety

RESULT: PC #407 SKY BLUE OVER NATURAL WOOL

¼ tsp. PC #407 Sky Blue over ½ yard presoaked natural wool

While it is nice to know how to dye a completely solid piece of fabric, rug hookers often prefer wool that is mottled: wool with both high and low values in the same piece. The combination of light and dark spots can hook up with more life than a single, flat value with no variation. Such variation gives a little pop to whatever is being hooked.

Less water in the pot restricts the ability of the wool's folds to open up and receive the dye. With less stirring during the dye process, those folds get set in place in the bath and are less available to receive the dye. Less wait time for the addition of citric acid (it actually goes in before the dye) speeds up the whole process, allowing dye to start penetrating as soon as the wool hits the bath.

Steam Punk Scroll, 16" round table mat, solid color mottled wool appliqué and colored thread on a solid color wool backing. Designed by Gene Shepherd, Anaheim, California; appliqué by Emily Gail Wyett, Huntington Beach, California, 2012.

The mottled wool gives just enough subtle variation in each of the fabrics to create a little extra interest on these sawtooth scrolls.

Step 1: For a ½-yard batch of wool fabric, start with a large pot that is only about one-third full of clear, boiling water. Mix up ¼ tsp. dye (PC #407 in this case) in a measuring cup of boiling water. Once completely dissolved, add it to the pot as described in batch 1. Stir with a long-handled spoon or set of tongs to make sure the dye is incorporated.

Solid Color with Mottling

Step 2: Turn off the heat. Measure 1 scant Tbsp. of citric acid crystals or a generous 1/2 cup of white vinegar and add it to the dye pot. Turning off the heat source is important since dye baths, particularly those in hard water, like to foam up and boil over with the addition of citric acid. While the water may still foam this way, with the heat off, it should not boil over the side of the pot. Stir the big pot with a big spoon to ensure that all additives are incorporated. With both citric acid and dye in the pot, the wool will immediately begin to accept the dye once it hits the water.

Step 3: Remove 1/2 yard of presoaked wool from its bath and wring out the excess water. Turn the heat source back on and, once the dye mixture begins to boil, dump the wool into the pot. In this method, you can scrunch up the wool and drop it in all at once. In fact, that helps give a mottled effect. Once it is in the dye bath, however, use a pair of sturdy tongs to give the wool a quick swish or stir to ensure that every bit of fabric comes in contact with some dye. Otherwise, there may be some white spots on the finished fabric.

Step 4: After that initial stir, let the wool sit in the dye bath and simmer unmolested. The more it is left alone, the more mottled it will be; stir it more, and it will have less mottling. Set the timer for 1 hour, cover the pot with a lid, and turn the heat down to a simmer. If you are concerned that the piece might have too much strong mottling, give the wool a gentle stir every 2 or 3 minutes as it cooks.

Step 5: Even though the wool will appear to have taken up the dye in about 20 minutes of cook time, it will still need to simmer for the entire hour in order for the dye to completely set. While the water may look clear, some colors (red in particular) never seem to completely go away. Sometimes a little extra citric acid and a little hotter cooking temperature help to facilitate this process.

These photos of batch 1 (solid color with no mottling) and batch 2 (solid color with mottling) illustrate the difference that water amounts, space limitations, and stirring make to the look of the finished product. Each technique used the same amount of wool and dye, yet the end results are quite different. It is not that one is right and the other wrong; it's all about the end result you want to achieve with your dye session.

Fall Oak Leaf Runner, *12½" x 31½", #6- and 8-cut wool on monk's cloth. Designed and hooked by Gene Shepherd, Anaheim, California, 2005.*

The background of this piece was hooked with mottled wool that had a medium amount of markings—similar to the amount of markings on the Sky Blue piece that introduced this batch.

Chinese Scroll, *34½" x 20½", #5- and 6-cut wool on monk's cloth. Designed by Anne Ashworth; hooked by Florence Lipar, Rancho Palos Verdes, California, 2012.*

Except for the dark navy outline, Florence used all mottled wool for this project. Even so, the two blues and the gray have much less mottling than their golden companion. This is because the blue and gray wool pieces were stirred more frequently during the cooking process than the gold.

Mottled Yarn

Just as subtle variation looks good in fabric, so too does it look good in yarn.

Step 1: Soak a 4-ounce skein of white or natural yarn as described in chapter 1.

Step 2: Put 2 to 3 inches of clear water in a medium dye pot. Turn on the heat and bring the water to a boil.

Step 3: As described in previous sections, mix up the amount of dye needed for the value of color you want to produce and add it to the pot. (A scant $1/8$ tsp. will produce a medium dark value; $1/32$ tsp. will produce a very light value; etc.) Add the citric acid, and stir the pot to incorporate.

Step 4: Before adding the yarn to the mixture, do an extra good job of wringing out the excess water so that the yarn is light and fluffy. As with fabric, scrunch up the yarn before inserting it into the dye bath.

Gently place the bundle on top of the simmering bath. Much of the yarn will slowly slip down into the bath, gently opening up to the dye as it does. The parts of yarn in the bath the longest will soak up the most color; those in for less time will soak up less. With only 2 to 3 inches of water in the pot, some of the yarn should remain above the bath, like the top of an iceberg. Let it sit that way for a couple minutes. If you need to stop that slow descent, do so with your tongs. Grab a section of the wool and lock the tongs, positioning them so the wool stays above the water until you are ready for it to slip into the bath. The longer the yarn stays out of the water, the lighter it will be because submerged sections of yarn will claim more of the dye, leaving less to go around when the top yarn finally slips beneath the surface.

As dye conditions are always a little different from pot to pot, there is no set amount of time to leave the yarn sticking out of the water. When your eye tells you it is the right time—certainly *before* the water starts to clear—use the tongs to poke the undyed yarn under the bath. Once again, you will need to make sure that all the white yarn comes in contact with the dye bath for long enough to get rid of all white spots. If you want a lot of variation, wait 2 or more minutes before submerging the yarn. If you want less variation, push the yarn down after 1 minute.

Cover the pot and keep the heat on a simmer for 1 hour. With only 3 inches of water in the pot, you will need to add more water so that the pot will not burn dry. Wait to add that water, however, until the yarn has taken up the color and the remaining water is clear. If maximum mottling is your goal, don't stir it at all. If less mottling is desired, give the pot a light stir every 6 to 8 minutes.

Appliqué ornament designed and made by Ruth Locke, Nipomo, California, 2011.

A big part of this ornament's appeal is the mottled look of the wool.

▲▲▲

Rug hookers often prefer wool that is mottled: wool with both high and low values in the same piece. The combination of light and dark spots can hook up with more life than a single, flat value with no variation. Such variation gives a little pop to whatever is being hooked.

▲▲▲

Tea Cozy, knitted by Alanah Shuck, Anaheim, California, 2012.

Two separate 4-ounce skeins of yarn were dyed with the solid color with mottling method to produce the wool needed for this tea cozy. The darkest value was made by using a generous $1/8$ tsp. of dye. The lighter value used a scant $1/32$ tsp. Although the variation in each skein was not severe, there are enough highs and lows to give each value a lot more interest than if it had been a solid, flat color. Each value received a bit of a sparkle.

It takes very little effort, along with little water and little stirring, to make yarn that has a lot of personality.

About Sheep

Making good wool is hard work. Don't be fooled, this Cheviot ewe is not resting; she is busy making good wool known for its resilience and durability. These traits make the breed a perfect choice for strong wool that can stand up to the tough demands whipped edges face.

Where would fiber artists be without sheep? Where, in particular, would I be without these specific Cheviot and Black-Faced Suffolk sheep, as they are the ones who provide me with the wool yarn I use to whip my hooked rugs?

For 50 years, Wilfrid (shown) and Jean Taylor, like all good shepherds, have lovingly cared for their flock at the Maple Terrace Farm, Saltspring Island, British Columbia, Canada. All of the whipping wool shown in this book came from the happy sheep at this family-owned farm.

Photos by David Pearson

DYEING WITH COMMERCIAL ACID DYE

batch 3

Overdyeing Colored Wool

▲▲▲

If you want lots of variation but need to hold the reins on time and money, try overdyeing more than one color of off-bolt fabric in a single dye bath.

▲▲▲

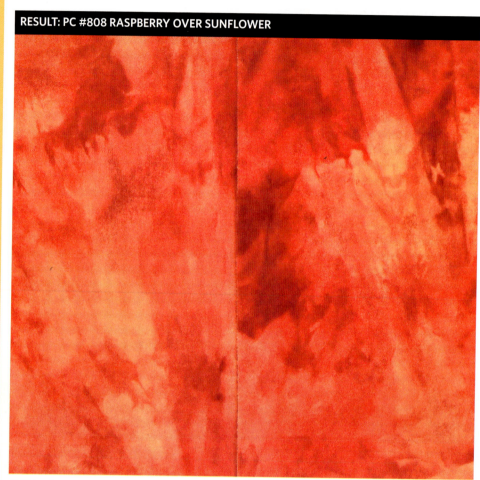

RESULT: PC #808 RASPBERRY OVER SUNFLOWER

Tahitian Sunset: Dorr's Sunflower wool overdyed with PC #808 Raspberry

Ways to Use Over-Dyed, Off-Bolt Wool

- Backgrounds with automatic variety
- Wool for grasses, tree canopies, and any application where different, yet related, wools are needed
- Any area where a wool with surprise colors is needed
- Repurposing small pieces of wool or leftover cuts

Just about any dye process that can be done over white or natural wool can be done over colored wool. Because many manufacturers offer wool fabric in a variety of stock colors by the yard, this dyeing option is great for home dyers. In addition to the beautiful end results, it's also an economical method for both time use and dollars as different looks can be created in one dye session.

Wool fabric dyed this way will be different depending on the color of the host wool. However, even vastly different colors of off-bolt wool become "related" once they come in contact with the same dye bath, making this method a great way of repurposing or incorporating all sorts of odd pieces.

Prodded Keet, *8½" x 14", #8- and 10- cut and shaped wool on primitive linen. Designed and hooked by Gene Shepherd, 2009.*

All the wool in the background of this piece was dyed with PC #808 Raspberry, two values over natural and one value over off-bolt Sunflower. Although made from the same simple dye color, two very different, yet related colors were produced to make dark, medium, and hot sections of the tropical background.

Version 1: Overdyeing One Color of Wool

Step 1: The initial steps for this batch are the same as those for the methods previously discussed. Instead of natural wool, however, use four 1/4-yard pieces of presoaked Dorr Sunflower wool. This method seems to work best in a pot that has less water, so the wool has less room to open up. For 1 yard of wool, fill a medium pot approximately half full of water.

Step 2: Once the water comes to a boil, turn off the heat and add the dissolved dye (1/2 tsp. PC #808 Raspberry in 1 cup boiling water) followed immediately by 1 tsp. citric acid granules. In my studio, the combination of mixed dye and citric acid usually produces an immediate rush of iridescent foam, as shown in this photo. If you add the mixed dye and citric acid to boiling water over an active heat source, the pot immediately boils over the side of the pot, taking the foam with it. To avoid this, always turn the heat off before adding both dye and citric acid. This foam can be a bit tricky, but remember that its unexpected effects are our friend! Think of it as the browned meat drippings in the bottom of the roast pan. Those drippings are important to good gravy; so, too, is foam important to dyed wool.

Step 3: With all four pieces of the wool in hand, return the heat source to high and wait until the bath starts to boil and foam. The moment the foam begins to rear its snarling head, drop in the wool. Wool seems to be the sacrifice the foam wants and, with its addition, things get back to normal in the pot. Wool soaked in a wetting agent does an even better job of taming the foam beast.

All about Foam

It took me a while to figure out that not all home dyers get the wonderful foam in their dye baths that I usually get. Since I love my foam and the surprise colors that show up as a result, you can imagine my consternation when doing dye demos on the road in a kitchen where no amount of coaxing could produce that foamy substance. Finally, with the help of an organic chemist, we discovered that foam shows up big in hard water and not at all in soft water. At my studio, I have very hard water. Consequently, I usually have a lot of foam during the initial moments of any dye process. For dyers who do not have hard water but want foam, you can turn water *hard* by adding these ingredients to one gallon of water:

▲ Epsom salts: 1/20 tsp.
▲ Calcium carbonate (lime, chalk): 1/334 tsp.

Since the average home dyer does not have a 1/334 tsp. measuring device, suffice it to say that in 1 to 2 gallons of water, you only need to add, in precise scientific terms, an itty bitty bit to make the water hard enough to interact with the dye in a foamy fashion.

I allow peaks of wool to remain above the dye bath for 30 to 45 seconds to encourage a good mottled effect. After that amount of time, all the wool gets a quick swish and is pushed under the waterline.

Regardless of when the wool is pushed under the dye, give it at least one good stir to make sure that all the wool makes contact with the bath. Once again, little stirring produces more mottling; more stirring produces less mottling. Don't be afraid to leave the wool alone as it cooks.

One other great side effect of a foamy bath is the dye scum that forms on the side of the pot. In this case, scum is our friend.

Before the water in the dye bath gets completely clear, particularly if you like splotchy wool, grab a tongful of wool and scrub down the sides of the pot so that the color in the scum is transferred to the wool. I usually clean one section of the pot with one piece of wool and a different section with another so as to distribute the foam residue to more than one piece. As foam is good for adding extra bits of additional color, so is scum. Once the sides are scrubbed down, cover the pot and cook the wool for 1 hour.

By way of review, this is what PC #808 Raspberry, in two different strengths, looks like when dyed over natural wool following the directions for batch 2: Solid Color with Mottling.

RESULT: PC #808 RASPBERRY OVER NATURAL WOOL

 TIP — **LESS AND MORE**

Less stirring = more mottling.
More stirring = less mottling.

Overdyeing Colored Wool

RESULT: PC #808 RASPBERRY OVER SUNFLOWER

This is what PC #808 Raspberry looks like when dyed over off-bolt yellow (Dorr Sunflower) wool. Everything but the host wool is the same. I call #808 over Sunflower wool "Tahitian Sunset."

Let's do it again with a different color. Following the same exact method as described above, this time I used ½ tsp. of PC #713 Olive Drab to overdye a yard of Dorr's Sunflower wool.

RESULT: PC #713 OLIVE DRAB OVER SUNFLOWER

When finished, PC #713 Olive Drab over yellow wool is anything but drab. Although the general formula of ½ tsp. to 1 yard was used for this batch, you could easily up the amount of dry dye from ½ tsp. to 1 tsp. to make a much darker version. Using less dye (¼ tsp.) would produce fabric that was much lighter.

Version 2: Overdyeing Multiple Colors of Wool

Why stop with one color? Instead of just using one color of off-bolt wool, why not add other colors to the same pot in order to create beautiful one-pot wonders? All the rest of the examples in this section will use four different ¼-yard pieces of Dorr off-bolt wool in each batch: Marigold, Morning Glory, Mint, and Sunflower.

The four base wools used to produce the results in this section: Dorr's Marigold, Morning Glory, Mint, and Sunflower.

As before, I measured and cut, presoaked, and finally cooked the wool for 1 hour in its respective dye bath made with ½ tsp. of dye.

TIP POPS OF COLOR

Want to add some unexpected pops of color to your dye batch? During the cooking, use the wool to scrub down the sides of the dye pot to transfer the foam scum to your wool.

Once again, 1/2 tsp. of PC #808 Raspberry dye was used over the total of 1 yard of wool in four 1/4-yard pieces each of Dorr's Marigold, Morning Glory, Mint, and Sunflower.

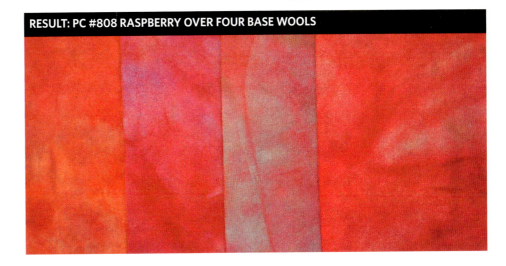

RESULT: PC #808 RASPBERRY OVER FOUR BASE WOOLS

Here is how the same four pieces look when overdyed with 1/2 tsp. PC #733 Ivy.

RESULT: PC #733 IVY OVER FOUR BASE WOOLS

This bath used 1/2 tsp. PC #122 Mustard over the same four colors of off-bolt wool. It produces a good color for a lion's mane. If cut, mixed, and used together for a background or a border, the pieces interact wonderfully. Additionally, if I wanted to hook a gold border or line to frame something, I could hook for a while with one piece, then transition to a second, eventually using all four colors to make that border. I could do this hit-or-miss or arrange the four pieces sequentially so that they make a natural gradation, one piece leading to the next.

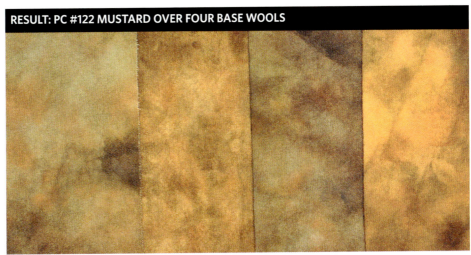

RESULT: PC #122 MUSTARD OVER FOUR BASE WOOLS

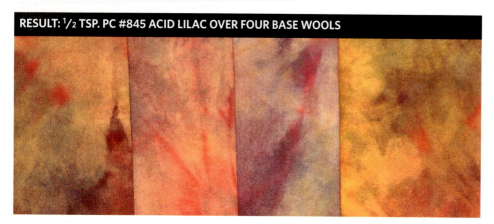

RESULT: ½ TSP. PC #845 ACID LILAC OVER FOUR BASE WOOLS

This is one of my favorite pairings: ½ tsp. PC #845 Acid Lilac over the four different pieces of wool. The end result is both surprising and pleasing.

RESULT: ¼ TSP. PC #845 ACID LILAC OVER FOUR BASE WOOLS

Notice the extreme difference between these pieces and the previous ones? All that I changed was the amount of dye. In this case, the dye amount was cut in half: ¼ tsp. PC #845 Acid Lilac over our same four colors of wool.

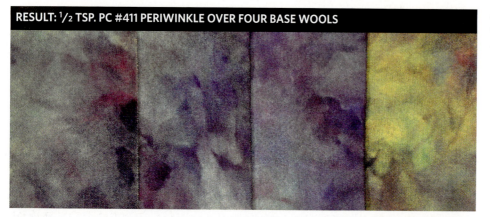

RESULT: ½ TSP. PC #411 PERIWINKLE OVER FOUR BASE WOOLS

Another particularly beautiful pairing is achieved with ½ tsp. PC #411 Periwinkle.

RESULT: ¼ TSP. PC #411 PERIWINKLE OVER FOUR BASE WOOLS

This is an example of the difference less dye (plus good foam and very little stirring) will make. This wool was produced with ¼ tsp. PC #411 Periwinkle over our four ¼-yard pieces.

Even over our four base pieces of off-bolt wool, there is still nothing drab about a dye bath of ½ tsp. PC #713 Olive Drab.

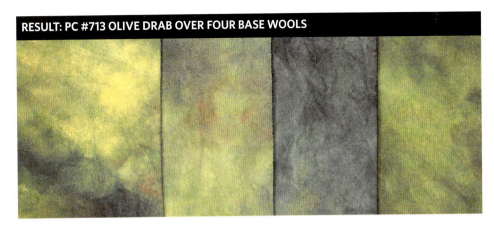

A bath of ½ tsp. of PC #503 Brown will unify other mixtures of colored wool in much the same way.

While ½ tsp. PC #508 Mahogany was used for this batch, increasing the amount to ¾ tsp. would take this look to an entirely different level.

Since I find interesting grays difficult to produce, I experimented with ½ tsp. PC #672 Jet Black over the same four pieces of colored wool. The end result produced grays with subtle overtones of each host wool.

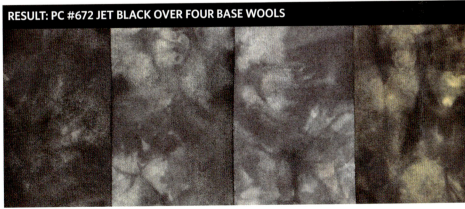

Why Not Worms?

BEFORE

AFTER

PC #733 Ivy was more than a match for that pan of multicolored cut strips. Now, they can have new life as a beautiful background.

If you think about it, leftover worm strips are nothing more than very small pieces of colored wool.

Cut strips can be overdyed with the same basic process, with these additional tips:

▲ Only overdye worms #6 cut and larger

▲ Because of their delicate nature, do not over-agitate them during any step of the dyeing process. Be gentle.

▲ Let the strips air dry on a flat surface

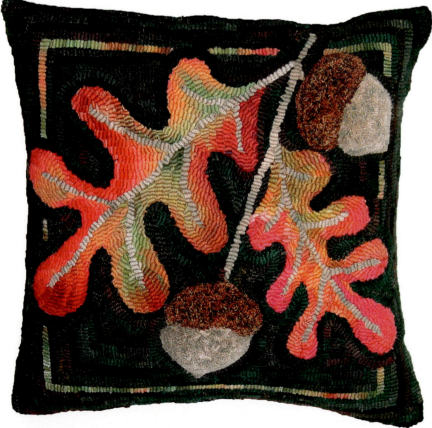

> **TIP** — **BUBBLING OVER**
>
> To stop foam from bubbling over when you add citric acid to your dye, turn the heat off first, mix in the acid crystals, then turn the heat back on.

Pickering Oak Leaf Pillow, *14" square, #8-cut wool on primitive linen. Designed and hooked by Gene Shepherd, Anaheim, California, 2006.*

The dark green background for this pillow was made by combining two colors of dye: 1 tsp. PC #713 plus $1/64$ tsp. PC #351. This recipe was then used to overdye $1/4$ yard. each of Dorr's Sunflower, Mint, #101, natural, and a pink that is no longer in production. Should you wish an even darker version, add a little more dye to the initial mix.

44 Prepared to Dye

DYEING WITH COMMERCIAL ACID DYE

Lazy Swatches

batch 4

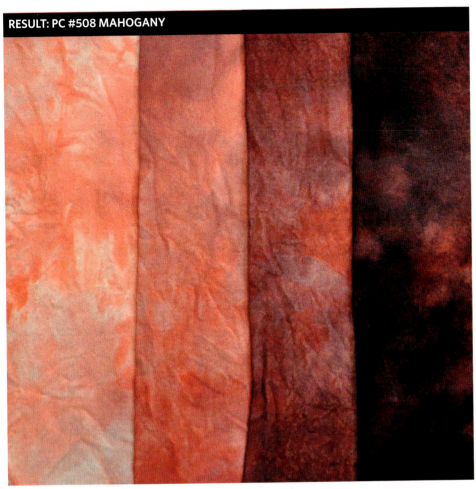

RESULT: PC #508 MAHOGANY

½ tsp. PC #508 Mahogany over four ¼-yard pieces natural wool

▲▲▲

Lazy is as lazy does. This method won't produce four pure values of the dye color, but you'll get a harmonious progression with subtle twists and turns not found in traditional methods.

▲▲▲

Lazy swatch wool is a quick, one-pot method for producing four or five values of one dye color. It is particularly good for any application where a non-fussy gradation is useful. The variation in value is easily achieved by staggering the addition of wool to the dye pot.

When making this sort of wool, remember that nearly all bought dye colors are achieved by mixing various amounts of the primary colors. Because colors go into the wool at different times in the cooking process (red goes first, blue is second, and yellow is the last), a staggered addition of wool pieces will produce some color variations as well. The last two pieces in the pot, for example, won't find as much red to gobble up as the early pieces did. So while everything that comes out of the pot will certainly go together, there are sure to be subtle differences between pieces based on the order in which they entered the dye pot. I find the results of this process much more interesting than those produced by traditional multivalue swatches.

Ways to Use Lazy Swatches

▲ Simple shaded projects
▲ Flowers with a more primitive look
▲ Leaves
▲ Scrolls
▲ Log Cabin geometrics
▲ In any project that needs multiple values of single colors

Lazy Swatches 45

Serene Selen (detail), 3' x 5', #6-cut wool strips on monk's cloth. Designed and hooked by Gene Shepherd, Anaheim, California, 2009. The yellow, green, blue, and purple families of wool used in this piece were all made with the lazy swatch method.

Version 1: Four Values of Plain Wool

Step 1: Prepare four 1/4-yard pieces of wool in either the short or long cut. Although I typically use natural wool when dyeing robust greens, golds, and blues, delicate pinks or other delicate colors that could be thrown off by a host that is not pure white demand the use of white wool. Presoak.

Step 2: Mix 1/2 tsp. dye in 1 cup boiling water. PC #508 Mahogany was used for this particular batch. For most colors, 1/2 tsp. dye to 1 yard of wool seems to be the right ratio. That combination provides a good four-value range from medium dark to fairly light wool when the dye chosen is a fairly robust color. (If you want even stronger values, use 3/4 tsp. dye.) However, some dyes start out more pale than others, particularly some soft yellows, apricots, and greens. If you desire four values from colors like that, either add a little more dye or use three pieces of wool instead of four.

Step 3: Bring a medium-sized pot, half full of water, to a boil. Turn off the heat, and add the cup of dissolved dye and the citric acid. For wool with fewer mottled splotches, use more water in the pot. Turn the heat back on, and bring the dye to a boil.

Once the dye bath begins to boil, immediately drop in one 1/4-yard piece of pre-soaked natural or white wool, swishing it just enough to make sure that all of the wool comes in contact with the dye. The biggest problem with this method occurs when the wool is not given this initial stir.

Extra Pot on Deck

When making a Lazy Swatch, it is a good idea to have a little saucepan of clear water and Synthrapol simmering away nearby to provide a resting place for pieces that are getting too much dye. When this situation arises, use your tongs to remove that piece to the extra pot where it can continue to cook and set without soaking up more dye.

Be Prepared to Whip

With the Lazy Swatch method, it's easy to include a small amount of yarn at any value-step you want. This foresight will provide whipping yarn in the exact colors used in projects made with lazy swatch wool. (See chapter 1 on how to prep and measure yarn.)

The 1/2 tsp. format given earlier for this batch can easily accommodate a small extra amount of yarn. Should you want yarn in more than one value, insert half of the skein when adding piece two and the rest when adding piece three. (Be careful not to catch the yarn hanging out of the pot on fire!) This stepped addition will give your yarn a decided two-value look. If you need a little more yarn for a bigger rug, then just add a little bit more dye by using a rounded teaspoon of dye to make the initial bath.

Failure of the wool to connect with the dye results in white spots that didn't soak up any dye. I realize that terms such as *swishing* and *initial stir* don't sound very precise. Just as you would give a tablecloth a good shake to remove crumbs, so too, in the dye bath, does the dyer need to give the wool a good shake so that it can completely open up and receive some dye. Once opened up, however, it can settle and sit as it soaks in the same fashion as in batch 2. It is important that the dye bath be boiling when each wool piece is added to the pot. The combination of heat and citric acid facilitate quick color pickup.

Once that swish movement is accomplished, keep the single piece of wool under the surface level of the dye bath by placing the tongs on top of the wool. This additional encouragement helps make the first piece the darkest.

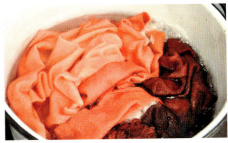

Step 4: After the initial piece cooks for about 35 to 40 seconds, toss in the second piece, stirring just enough to make sure all the wool comes in contact with the dye bath. Of course, if no splotches are desired, additional stirring will ensure that the coloration will be smooth. Repeat this process every 35 to 40 seconds until four pieces of wool have been added to the pot.

While the staggered addition of wool usually provides four distinct values, you really need to let your eyes guide you on this one. Every pot is a little different. If piece number three, for example, seems to be getting a little dark, just use the tongs to remove it to a waiting saucepan for a few moments and let the other pieces catch up before returning it to the pot. If, once all four pieces of wool are in the pot, there does not seem to be quite enough dye left for the fourth piece, then remove the first three pieces for a little while to let the fourth hog up what dye is left in the pot until you think it looks right. If the fourth piece is really deprived, add 1/128 to 1/64 tsp. of dye to the pot to bring up the color level, then return the first three pieces. When judging by sight, remember that colors always look darker when wet.

After a few minutes of cooking, the wool pieces ought to clearly show a good gradation and the water ought to look fairly clear. Don't be surprised, however, if subtle changes take place during the complete hour-long cook time. Even clear water can still have trace amounts of color, which eventually go into the wool during the final simmer. By my way of thinking, that is a very good thing.

Step 5: When the appearance of the wool meets your standards, cover the pot with a lid, lower the heat to a simmer, and cook the wool for 1 hour to set.

Lazy Swatches

RESULT: PC #808 RASPBERRY

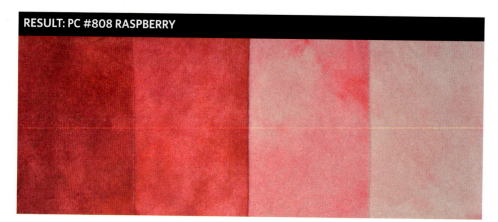

#808 Raspberry produces a cheery pink that works great for hooked or prodded flowers.

RESULT: PC #845 ACID LILAC

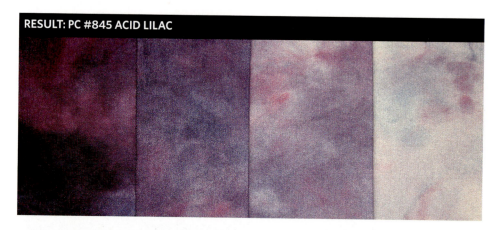

The lighter values of this grouping lend themselves to realistic prodded lilacs. The darker values make great hooked or appliqué grapes.

RESULT: PC #411 PERIWINKLE

A deep color like this could easily handle a fifth piece of wool.

RESULT: PC #713 OLIVE DRAB

When looking at the manufacturer's swatch, no one would ever guess that PC #713 Olive Drab would come out of the pot looking like this. Yet, through the magic of delayed pot entry, the pieces shimmer and glow with their own unique set of highlights.

When using soft colors like #709, add wool pieces in quicker succession in order to make sure each one gets enough dye.

This swatch was made with a mixture of dyes: 1/2 tsp. PC #707 Avocado plus 1/4 tsp. PC #123 Toffee.

PC #501 MochaChino is another dye color that produces striking contrasts.

Version 2: Lazy Swatch with Both Natural and Textured Wool

Version 1 was illustrated using four pieces of wool because that number consistently works with ½ tsp. of most any dye. Even so, there is nothing sacred about the number four, and a person could take one piece away or add a couple more to the staggered progression. I routinely add five or six pieces if I want my values to go fairly light. But there are more options available as well.

RESULT: PC #228 SAFFRON OVER NATURAL AND TEXTURED WOOL

It is even more enjoyable, when adding additional pieces of wool fabric to the pot, to include at least one piece of plaid or textured wool to each batch. Fiber artists want and need as much textured wool as they can get; this second version of the Lazy Swatch technique will help you create a ready supply in the colors of your choice.

Step 1: Prep five or six ¼-yard pieces of wool, including at least one piece of plaid/textured wool.

Step 2: Mix a heaping ½ tsp. dye in the color of your choice into 1 cup boiling water. If you are planning on dyeing six or seven pieces, add a bit more dye. PC #228 Saffron was used for this particular batch.

Step 3: Fill the dye pot two-thirds full of water, and bring it to a boil.

Step 4: Turn off the heat and add both the dye and the citric acid. Once incorporated, turn the heat on.

Step 5 (right): When the dye bath comes to a boil, add the first piece of natural wool, and treat it as described in the previous version. Never add a textured piece first. Since the first piece in always becomes the darkest piece, give that honor to a plain piece of wool. The textured piece, because it is constructed with some dark threads, will naturally end up looking darker than any of the solid colors. Although the sequence of dyed Saffron pieces shown above arranges the wool in value order, lightest to darkest, they weren't dyed in that order. The dark solid piece, second from the right, went in first and the plaid went in second. Values three, four, and five complete the swatch in both values and dyeing order.

 TIP — STIR TEXTURES MORE

Whenever you add a textured piece to a Lazy Swatch bath, do a little extra stirring. Textures often need a little help making contact with enough dye to make a difference in their look.

Step 6: Add textured pieces to the mix as pieces two and three. I usually don't add them at stages when the dye concentration will be at lesser levels. Too much dye will obliterate those textured markings, and too little dye will produce a piece that can't quite seem to make up its mind as to what color it is supposed to be.

Grandma Rayl Pillow, 13" square, #6-cut wool strips on linen. Designed by Gene Shepherd; hooked by Peggy Johnson, Los Angeles, California, 2012.
Except for the dark interior background, lazy swatches were used for all aspects of this project. Although all four green leaves were hooked in value order, two were hooked light to dark and the other two were hooked dark to light. Two of the log cabin corners were hooked in value order, light to dark to light, without any tweed, and two were hooked out of order with tweed. The flower was hooked to illustrate the simplified shading of a lazy swatch. Whether hooked in order or out of order, this method of dyeing gives the fiber artist many options.

Big Momma (detail), 6½' x 31", #9- and 10-cut wool on primitive linen. Adapted by Gene Shepherd from an original design by Marny Cardin; hooked by Gene Shepherd, Anaheim, California, 2009.

Just because four or five values of color are created in one dye pot does not mean that all values have to be used together. This big flower utilizes pieces from multiple color lazy swatches in both its purple and gold sections.

Prodded Flowers, 12" x 12", torn and shaped wool, prodded on synthetic homespun. Designed and prodded by Gene Shepherd, Anaheim, California, 2009.

In my opinion, flowers, whether hooked or prodded, always look better in values that are a bit unpredictable. Lazy swatch wool from two completely different swatches cooperated in these lilacs. Such variation gives the piece additional realism. If prodding a rose, do the center in a dark value and then finish it with wool from the next darkest piece. Leaves always look better when darker values are prodded close to the blossoms, followed with medium shades and then a few of the lightest ones to finish. To make flowers like this, all you need is a good book on the topic (Prodded Hooking for a Three-Dimensional Effect is a good choice) and some lazy swatch wool!

Serene Selen (detail), designed and hooked by Gene Shepherd.

Why hook a striking puzzle line in one color value when three graduated colors from a lazy swatch will give the undulating line even more movement?

DYEING WITH COMMERCIAL ACID DYE

Traditional Multivalue Swatches

batch 5

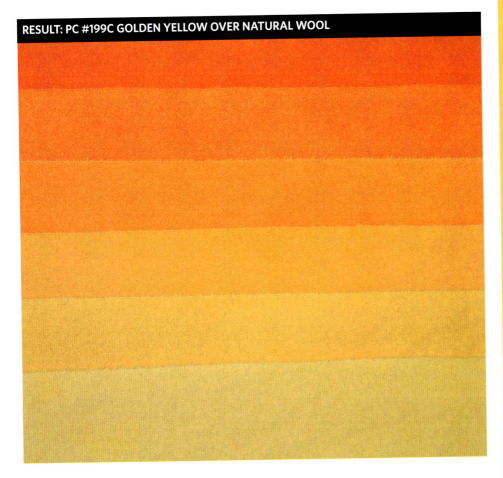

RESULT: PC #199C GOLDEN YELLOW OVER NATURAL WOOL

▲▲▲

For smooth transitions from one value to another, nothing beats traditional multivalue swatches.

▲▲▲

A traditional multivalue swatch produces a smooth gradation of true color in several different values, ranging from dark to light. This type of swatch is usually produced with at least 6 and as many as 12 pieces of wool. Multivalue swatches have long been associated with traditional floral patterns and any design or element that calls for fine shading. While this dye technique is considered very traditional, the colors used to make swatches certainly don't have to fit in that box.

Each piece of a multivalue swatch cooks alone in a single pot, guaranteeing that all color ingredients in any given dye mixture have the time to fully penetrate each piece of wool. Consequently, this method will produce true solid colors, in a variety of graduated values.

Ways to Use Multivalue Swatches

- Finely shaded flowers and scrolls
- Design elements that need to be depicted in a gradation of values of one pure color
- Any project that calls for multiple values of a single color

Persian Miniature (detail), 51" x 64", #3-, 4-, and 5-cut wool on monk's cloth. Designed by Pearl McGown; hooked by Florence Lipar, Ranchos Palos Verdes, California, 2012.

The leaves, scrolls, and flowers in this lovely piece were all hooked with traditional multivalue swatches.

Version 1: Gradation by Measurement

Cut and presoak six 1/8-yard pieces of white (or natural) wool. Since white wool is a neutral base for any color, it is always a good choice for multivalue swatches. Natural wool, which is not pure white, has just a hint of a yellowish beige color. While that little bit of pigment rarely shows up in most colors, natural wool can slightly skew delicate pinks and reds. Consequently, for colors in the red family, or if you are really particular about avoiding color contamination, use white. Since the color being shown in this example is in the yellow family, natural wool was a fine choice.

Step 1: Place 2 to 2 1/2 quarts of water in each of six pots. If you do not have the space or equipment to cook them all at once, then do it in stages. Turn on

the heat, and bring the water to a boil. Do not add citric acid yet.

Step 2: Choose any color of dye you wish. Use a commercial dye as is, or if you choose to reproduce your favorite dye color from a recipe book, multiply those directions to make a little more than 1/2 tsp. total of dry dye mixture. Place the dry dye in a juice glass or custard cup.

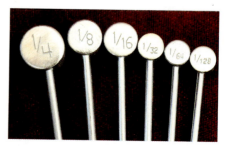

Step 3: Mix up six different batches using each of the following amounts of dye: 1/4 tsp., 1/8 tsp., 1/16 tsp., 1/32 tsp., 1/64 tsp., and 1/128 tsp. Since the total amount of dye used to make all 6 cups is just under 1/2 tsp., either commercial colors or your own special recipe will work as long as there is that much dye before you start measuring. Add 1 cup boiling water to each cup, and stir until all the dye powder is completely mixed.

Step 4 (top left): Add each mixture of dye to its own pot. In the front row, proceeding left to right, the pots contain dye in this order: ¼ tsp., ⅛ tsp., and ¹⁄₁₆ tsp.. The back three pots contain the remaining dye mixtures: from right to left, ¹⁄₃₂ tsp., ¹⁄₆₄ tsp., and ¹⁄₁₂₈ tsp. Even without any wool in the pot, it is obvious that these graduated measurements will produce graduated values.

Step 5: Dealing with one pot at a time, add a piece of wool to the boiling water. Stir the wool as it cooks. Wool that is stirred a lot will have an even coloration with no spots; wool left unattended will get spotty. Since swatches are usually made with no spots, plan on doing a lot of stirring. When the water starts to clear, add citric acid and continue to stir for 2 or 3 minutes. Now proceed to the second pot and dye another piece of wool as you did for pot one.

Step 6 (top right): Each pot of wool needs to cook for 1 full hour after the citric acid has been added. Although it is not necessary to continually stir each pot the entire time, which would be rather hard to do unless you have six hands, give each pot a quick stir every few minutes. Add a little boiling water to each cooking pot whenever water levels get low.

When completely cooked, the wool is a wonderful gradation in six values of pure color.

Mitzi's Tulips, 20" x 43½", #4-, 5-, and 6-cut wool on cotton rug warp. Designed by Gene Shepherd; hooked by Florence Lipar, Rancho Palos Verdes, California, 2012.

The six-value Golden Yellow Swatch was used to shade the golden yellow tulips in this piece. Each of the other tulips was made with dip dyes.

Version 2: Gradation by Pouring

RESULT: MAJIC CARPET RED VIOLET OVER WHITE WOOL

With the pouring method, you can dye lighter pieces as long as each dilution provides enough pigment to visibly affect the wool. Twelve pieces were made in this grouping from $1/2$ tsp. of dye.

Since not everyone has a complete set of dye spoons, here is a version that makes it possible to get a multivalue swatch with just one measuring spoon. It is the version I use to make swatches with 8 to 12 values. If you can measure and pour water in a measuring cup, this is the version for you.

Although the example in the following steps was made with $1/2$ tsp. dye, any amount of dye in the initial mixing vessel will work. Measurements of more than $1/2$ tsp. dye will, of course, create pieces in deeper values while measurements of less dye will result in lighter values. This method allows for any reasonable measurement.

Step 1: Presoak 12 pieces of white wool fabric, each $1/8$ yard in size.

Step 2: You will need both a 2-cup and a 1-cup measure for this version as well as $1/2$ tsp. of dry dye. I used Majic Carpet Red Violet. Place $1/2$ tsp. dry dye in the 2-cup vessel.

Step 3: Carefully pour 2 cups boiling water in the bigger vessel. Be exact! Stir the mixture until all the dye is incorporated.

Step 4: From the 2-cup measure, pour 1 cup mixed dye solution into the 1-cup vessel. Since the first cup started out with $1/2$ tsp. of dye, now that it is split into two equal batches, each contains $1/4$ tsp. of dye, which is the amount of dye used for the darkest value in version 1.

Storing Mixed Dyes

Whether it is mixtures from a several-value swatch session that you didn't have burners for when you mixed the dye, leftover dye from another project, or dye that you would like to mix up a day or so before a big dye session, any mixed dye can be stored and saved until you are ready for it. Just make sure you follow these guidelines.

1. Place any amount of premixed dye you wish to save in a glass jar with a tight-fitting lid. This is a perfect opportunity to recycle condiment and jam jars. Just make sure that once you start using them as dye containers they stay in your dye kitchen and do not get rotated back into your home kitchen.

2. Label the top of each jar with the dye color and approximate strength/amount of dye. This is particularly important if you are making up dye before a session.

3. If storing for more than 8 hours, keep all jars of dye in a refrigerator. While it is true that dye often lasts longer than that, depending on room temperature, I don't always get back to my dye when I think I am going to. I've had dye mold when stored at room temperature, so I always stick my saved jars of dye in a dedicated little fridge until I am ready for them.

4. If you are storing dye for several days or weeks, make a habit of shaking each jar once or twice a week. Undisturbed dye can settle and separate. Remixing it every so often with a good shake helps avoid that problem (as well as illustrating why tight-fitting lids are a must). I don't suggest keeping dyes for longer than a month.

5. Before using, give the jar a very good shake. If some dye separation is still apparent, add a little bit of boiling water and shake or stir some more before adding to your dye pot.

Take the 1-cup vessel to a waiting pot of boiling water. Turn off the heat. Pour the entire cup of dye solution into the pot and stir well **(top left)**. Do not add citric acid yet.

Turn the heat back on. Once the bath begins to boil, add one piece of soaked wool. The wool needs to be stirred a lot to ensure a smooth coloration with no spots. Follow the same instructions as before, stirring until the water clears. Now add the citric acid.

Step 5 (top right): Go back to the original 2-cup measuring cup, which is now half full (in strength, it's equal to $1/4$ tsp. dye) and add enough boiling water to bring the level back to the 2-cup mark.

Stir it well, and pour out 1 cup of this new mixture into the empty 1-cup vessel. Half of this second batch equals $1/8$ tsp. of dye, which is also half as strong as the first pot of wool. This new outpouring of dye can go to a new pot and a new piece of wool. Add and stir as described.

Step 6: After each cup is poured out for a new dye pot, top off the original 2-cup vessel with water to bring the level back to the 2-cup mark.

Proceed in this fashion whether you are making 6 or 12 values of wool. Each successive batch will be half as strong in value as the previous one, as illustrated below.

Traditional Multivalue Swatches 57

You can keep pouring, dyeing, and topping off the original dye cup as long as you have burners available to cook the batch. The original ½ tsp. of dye used in this particular version was poured, topped off, and poured again as described to make twelve ⅛-yard values of Red Violet.

If all your burners are full before the desired number of batches are cooking in their pots, don't stop measuring. Use some extra pint jars to contain as many successive dilutions as desired. Once a measurement is poured, cap it for another time when burners are available. I recommend doing the measuring, pouring, and capping in one session—even if you know you aren't going to cook all the separate little batches that day. That way, if you have to wait one day or one week before the next session, all you need to remember is that the correct measurements of dye have been prepared and are ready for the wool. As long as the measured dye is kept in the refrigerator in an airtight container, the dye will be ready when you are.

What About Swatches?

A traditional multivalue swatch produces a smooth gradation of true color in several different values, ranging from dark to light. Multivalue swatches have long been associated with traditional floral patterns and any design or element that calls for fine shading.

Although making a traditional multivalue swatch is easy, many people prefer to buy them from professional suppliers. Following precise recipes applied in a regimented and systematic way, suppliers offer a line of colors that stay true from batch to batch. All fiber artists know that dye lots can vary slightly from batch to batch, so if you need one more swatch to finish a rug that has already used four, your best bet for getting a close match is to get it from the original supplier.

Swatches come in a rainbow of colors. This is just a small sampling of Jane Olson's 75 stock colors, 50 of which came from the McClain (Cox) swatch line, which was bought by Jane Olson in 1979. During her career, Jane added the other 25 stock colors, all of which are still being made by her granddaughter, Brigitta Phy.

A 1/16-yard piece (yellow) is approximately three times bigger than the average piece (blue) from a commercial swatch. Therefore, if you are making a swatch with 1/16-yard pieces, the end result will be equal to three commercial swatches.

Some Reflection on Swatch Tweaking

All the directions for making traditional multivalue swatches have emphasized the need for frequent stirring so you do not end up with splotchy swatches. That is how it has been traditionally done—and what is necessary—if one wants to produce that smooth, expected, gradual gradation where one value melts into the other. However, I must confess that I am usually attracted to wool that is not so predictable.

Therefore, on the rare occasions when I make multivalue swatches for myself—or a friend with similar rebellious leanings—I stir less and end up with values that are a little blotchy. I think this replicates the look of flowers in my wife's garden better, as nature rarely does anything without blushing. I am not advocating one sort of swatch over another—just remember that even something as traditional as a swatch can be tweaked a bit if it suits your taste or needs.

Finally, as one who never does anything small or in multiples if it can be done all at once, I always make more swatch wool than I think I will need. Particularly with this method, where the end result can vary due to something as slight as changes within the city water system, it is better to have leftovers than to be scrambling to make more because you ran out. For that reason, I never use swatch wool pieces smaller than $1/16$ yard, which is half the size of the pieces ($1/8$ yard) used to demonstrate this batch.

Maytime (detail), #4- and 5-cut wool strips on rug warp. Designed by Jane Olson; hooked by Brigitta Phy, Sebastopol, California, 2011.
Nothing matches the look of a multivalue swatch when a traditional shaded look is the goal. Jane Olson would be proud of her granddaughter's meticulous work.

DYEING WITH COMMERCIAL ACID DYE

batch 6

▲▲▲
A little time and effort lead to big surprises and unique gradations—all in one strip.
▲▲▲

Ways to Use Dip Dyes

Dip-dyed wool is perfect for any project where a single strip with one light-to-dark gradation is wanted.

- ▲ Leaves
- ▲ Scrolls
- ▲ Skies
- ▲ Cat's Paws
- ▲ Background, when cut against the selvedge

Dip Dyes

RESULT: PC #713 OLIVE DRAB OVER NATURAL

This dip-dyed piece of wool will allow for a smooth, seamless transition from very light to very dark olive in a hooked leaf or scroll.

Although dip dyes produce the same light-to-dark value gradation as swatches, they do so in one piece of wool instead of four or six separate pieces. This technique allows for the seamless transition of values so attractive in a leaf, piece of fruit, or scroll. Because the darker section of the fabric lies in the bath longer than the lighter sections, it takes on more of the colors in the dye, like the pieces in a lazy swatch. These surprise colors give the piece a tremendous vibrancy.

Giant Dahlia, 16" x 16", #5- and 8-cut wool strips on linen. Designed and hooked by Laura Pierce, Petaluma, California, 2009.
After outlining all the petals with a #5-cut of spot-dyed wool, the artist filled each one with #8-cuts from a dip dye. To get good variation in her petals, she created four or five dip dyes that each featured a different color: pale yellow, peach, pink, or purple. As the artist said: "It is really simple." As I say: "It is really simple if you have the right dip-dyed wool!"

Version 1: Dip Dye over White or Natural Fabric

Step 1: Presoak the wool as usual. I used natural wool for this version.

Step 2: Prepare a dye mixture that is appropriate for the piece of wool being dyed. I used $1/4$ tsp. of PC #713 Olive Drab for a $1/2$-yard piece of wool. Cut at 36 inches on selvedge.

Step 3: Fill a large pot two-thirds full of water, and bring it to a boil. Turn off the heat and add the dye. You can add the citric acid now for a splotchier dip dye; for smoother transitions, delay the acid until after at least 3 minutes of dipping. Stir well.

Step 4: Make a loose accordion fold with the wool, holding it securely in one hand. Turn the heat back on, and bring the pot to a boil.

To get an accurate reading on the strength of the dye bath, use a measuring cup to get a true sampling. The water always looks different in a measuring cup than it does in the pot. Although this is a weak bath, it would still overpower the light edge of this particular dip dye.

To force most of the color in the lower section of the fabric, use a pair of tongs to grasp the white end of the fabric fold at the top. Lock the tongs on that fold and roll up the wool so that the white part is held in the twist. Position the handle of the tongs in the handle of the pot so that the roll cannot come undone. This will allow the bottom section of the fabric to sit and soak a few extra minutes in the dye bath. Do not leave the wool in this position too long as a line of dye will form at the water level. Even if you need to reposition the tongs every 40 to 60 seconds, it is easier to work over the hot water with the tongs than with your hand.

Step 5: Begin dipping the wool in the pot in an up-and-down, bobbing motion. Constant dipping and bobbing accomplish the same thing in this method as continual stirring does in previous methods. Don't immerse the entire piece at the beginning of this step. Start by bobbing about 8 to 12 inches for 1 to 2 minutes, then increase it to a depth of 12 to 16 inches. I often bob the wool up and down four or five times, then plunge 6 inches deeper with a quick plunge before returning to a lesser amount for five or six more plunges. Every 1 to 2 minutes, transfer the top accordion fold of the wool from one hand to the other, one inch or fold at a time. This will help spread out the wool in the pot so that it better absorbs the dye. Without the up-and-down motion, horizontal dye lines will form on the wool; without the side to side movement, vertical streaks will form in the folds of the wool. Although I don't mind a few lines—some applications even benefit from the vertical lines—the goal should be the smoothest gradation possible.

Take time with this process. The longer a section stays in the dye, the darker it will be. Sections that are kept out of the pot the most will, of course, end up being the lightest. There is always a temptation, particularly when it seems that most of the color has gone out of the pot, to drop the last of the strip in and be done. Avoid that temptation, as early entry will lessen the effect of the gradation.

Step 6: Before all of the dye has gone into the wool, the lightest ends of the strips should be dumped in the pot. Then stir the pot so that the fabric cannot rest. Resting fabric will end up being mottled; fabric on the move will not mottle. Set the timer and cook the wool for 1 hour, stirring frequently.

RESULT: PC #713 OLIVE DRAB OVER NATURAL WOOL

When you're ready to hook, a cut strip from this 34-inch finished piece of dip-dyed wool will create a smooth dark-to-light gradation for an 8-inch leaf or scroll.

Version 2: Dip Dye over Multiple Pieces of Colored Wool

Follow the same starting procedure through step 2 of version 1. In this example, I used $1/2$ tsp. of PC #819 Purple over $1/4$-yard pieces of Dorr Marigold, Sunflower, Morning Glory, and Natural.

Step 1: Presoak all colored pieces in a single bath of cool water for about 15 minutes. Wet pieces will dip and bob better than dry ones. If you are using natural or white wool as one of the colors, presoak either of them for the normal time.

Step 2: Assemble all the pieces in one hand with a loose accordion fold.

Step 3: Continue as in version 1.

Determine the Length for Your Dip-Dyed Wool

If you are dyeing wool to hook a specific project, measure the length your dip dye needs to cover and multiply by four. Generally speaking, it will take an 8-inch strip to hook a 2-inch line and a 36-inch strip to hook a 9-inch line. Because wool shrinks about 10% during dyeing and drying, add a little extra length to your final predye length. If you hook high loops, add even more.

Dip Dyes 63

RESULT: PC #819 PURPLE OVER MARIGOLD, SUNFLOWER, MORNING GLORY, AND NATURAL

Left: *Finished pieces for Version 2 are shown in this order: Marigold, Sunflower, Morning Glory, and Natural. This particular grouping would make good wool for hooked tulips. A couple of the pieces have a little vertical stripe because they weren't opened/transferred from side to side enough during the early stages of the process. Since these pieces are destined for tulips, such a little vertical blemish will work well. Should more stripes be desired, do most of the dip dye without letting go of the initial accordion fold.*

RESULT: PC #123 TOFFEE OVER MARIGOLD, SUNFLOWER, MORNING GLORY, AND NATURAL

RESULT: PC #713 OLIVE DRAB OVER SUNFLOWER, MINT, MORNING GLORY, AND MARIGOLD

Above: *These pieces are a good example of the mottling that will appear on the wool if you don't stir during the hour-long cook time. Made with PC #123 Toffee, this wool is certainly useable and, for some leaf projects, might even be more desirable than a smooth gradation. Stirring is just another way that the dye artist can manipulate the process to create the perfect wool for every setting.*

Left: *I created this batch of ¼-yard pieces (Sunflower, Mint, Morning Glory, and Marigold) in a dip dye bath of ½ tsp. of PC #713 Olive Drab. It was stirred regularly during the final cooking process. Because each host fabric dyes up a little differently than the others, such variation gives the artist more options than using only one kind of wool. Something as simple as hooking one side of a long leaf with cut strips of Marigold (right) and the other side with the much lighter Sunflower wool (left) will give the leaf greater depth than a single color fill. The same combination would also work well in a split-color appliqué leaf.*

Heart of the Home (detail; see the full rug on page 175).

To create a scrappy/primitive look for the scrolls in this design, I overdyed combinations of 1/4-yard (9-inch by the bolt width) pieces of white, natural, Mint, Sunflower, Morning Glory, and Marigold in separate batches of PC #121 Maple Sugar, #122 Mustard, #123 Toffee, and #124 Gold. Additional fabric, which included Dorr #101 (medium green), Mint, Morning Glory, and Gray Houndstooth, was also dip dyed with PC #822 Plum for the leaf sections of the scrolls.

Version 3: Color-Tipped Ends

RESULT: PC #713 OLIVE DRAB OVER SUNFLOWER, MORNING GLORY, MARIGOLD, AND MORNING GLORY, TIPPED WITH PC #719 GRASSHOPPER AND PC #808 RASPBERRY

Any dip dye can be tipped with a new color of dye before it goes into its final cooking stage.

Step 1: Follow every step for the production of a dip dye batch in the color of your choice with one exception: do not dye the lightest ends of the pieces; keep them in the jaws of the tongs.

Step 2: In a nearby pot, prepare a second color bath. If this is a dedicated bath meant just for the dip dye, the strength of dye in the bath should not be too strong. If tipping the ends of 1/2 yard of pieces, start with 1/64 tsp. When dipping, if that does not seem strong enough, add a little more dye until the proper strength is achieved. Add some citric acid, and bring the pot to a boil.

This batch of dip dye, like the examples shown in this section, was made with colored fabric in a bath of PC #713 Olive Drab. The difference, however, came at the very end of the process when the two pieces on the left were tipped in a bath of PC #719 Grasshopper and the two on the right were tipped in a bath of PC #808 Raspberry. I usually dye several pots, in multiple methods, at one time. Dyeing a lazy swatch of Raspberry on the next burner over from an Olive Drab dip dye allows me to tip the light end of the green in the berry for a spicy finish.

Heart of the Home, 12 1/2" x 17 1/2", #6-cut wool on primitive linen. Designed by Gene Shepherd; hooked by Iris Salter, Coarsgold, California, 2013.

The artist used yard-long pieces of color-tipped dip dyes to hook the 9-inch-long scrolls in this piece.

Purple Tip Dahlia, 12" x 12", #6-cut wool on linen. Designed and hooked by Laura Pierce, Petaluma, California, 2006.

To prepare the dip dyes for these petals, Laura measured the longest length in the design and multiplied by four to discover the approximate length of wool she would need to hook each one. (A 3-inch petal, for example, would take a minimum strip of 12 inches long, or 14 inches to be on the safe side.) Each piece of petal wool was made with white wool, dipping one end in Cushing Peacock Green and the other end in Cushing Blue Burgundy.

Step 3: When the first batch reaches its finish point in pot one, remove the wool and reverse the order of the pieces so that the dyed ends of the strips are secured in the jaws of a locking set of tongs. Begin dipping and bobbing the undyed tips of the wool in the new color. Start by dipping 6 to 10 inches of the wool, going a little deeper every sixth bob or so. A good blush, in reverse graduated order, is the goal.

It is important to bring a little of this new color into most of the strip so there is not one big line of abrupt color change. When it appears that most of the new color has gone into the ends of the pieces, all the wool can be put into the pot. Stir regularly during the hour-long cooking process to avoid mottling. At any time, if there is too much residual dye in a pot, you can finish cooking the dip dye in a pot of clear water with citric acid. You will, however, still need to stir.

Hooking Tips for Dip Dyes

Whether the cut piece of dip dye is 16, 34, or 50 inches long, you are not obligated to start hooking with either end of a piece, nor are you obligated to use all of a single piece every time you hook. Quite frequently, the color section needed for a certain spot is not conveniently on either end of the strip! When that is the case, pull a strip of the dip dye through the backing until the right color or value shows up. At that point begin to hook. All the long tails can be saved for other spaces. When you are hooking light to dark and the strip runs out before the dark line is completely filled, pick up another dark end and continue hooking until the dark spot is filled. You may have to rob two or three pieces of their dark ends to accomplish this. Dip dyes can be started, stopped, and spliced together in any way that will help you accomplish your goal. Remember, they work for you; you don't work for them.

Version 4: A Dip Dye Sky

RESULT: PC #407 SKY BLUE OVER WHITE WOOL

Since the horizon line is usually lighter than the top part of a sky, a dip dye is the perfect way to dye a sky.

Although the general instructions for this version are the same as those given for other versions, there are some special considerations.

- Use white wool.
- Use a deep steamer pan for this procedure instead of a pot. The width of such a pan facilitates the wool's need to spread out for a smooth gradation.
- A little dye goes a long way. I usually use $1/16$ tsp. of PC #407 Sky Blue for 1 yard of wool.
- Add citric acid late in the process.
- Stir frequently to minimize spotting.

After the cook time, be sure to let the sky colors cool down in the pan before rinsing.

> **TIP — ACID MOMENT**
>
> If you want the smoothest gradation possible, delay adding citric acid until several minutes into the dip-dyeing process. Should a more mottled gradation be your goal, add the citric acid at the beginning.

Prairie Blooms, 28" x 36", #6- and 7-cut and hand torn/shaped proddy pieces on linen. Designed by Mary Lynn Gehrett and Gene Shepherd; hooked and prodded by Mary Lynn Gehrett, 2011.

Although the wool used to hook this horizontal directional sky was not four times longer than the width of the piece, by hooking the pieces sequentially, in the order they were cut, all the natural gradation of the original fabric was kept together in the final product.

▲▲▲
Dip dyes allow for the seamless transition of values so attractive in a leaf, piece of fruit, or scroll. These surprise colors give the piece a tremendous vibrancy.
▲▲▲

| TIP | **COLOR GONE** |

If you fear all the dye might be soaked up before the ends get dipped, plunge the ends in the pot and open the tongs. Allow the wool to open enough for the wool to take up a little color. Then the light ends can once again be caught with the tongs and removed so the bottom can continue to cook until you are ready to add the top of the wool.

Prepared to Dye

DYEING WITH COMMERCIAL ACID DYE

Jelly Roll

batch 7

RESULT: PC #508 MAHOGANY OVER MARIGOLD AND PC #713 OLIVE DRAB OVER NATURAL WOOL

Two of these pieces were dyed over Dorr Marigold wool with PC#508 Mahogany. The center piece is natural wool dyed with PC #713 Olive Drab.

▲▲▲
No other technique gives the dyer as much control over the outcome as this one.
▲▲▲

This is an interesting technique that can be done in a variety of ways. While it could be used to prepare unique wool for rug hooking, the end result, because it is so pretty and the process so labor-intensive, seems better suited for applications where the wool can be seen in its entirety. This is one of those techniques where the saying is true: it is so pretty that it would be a shame to cut it.

Ways to Use Jelly Roll Wool

- Neck scarves
- Appliqué embellishments
- Pillow borders and backings
- As a base for hooked and prodded projects
- Hooked projects that require an unusual stripe

Although the jelly roll technique can be done with wool in almost any size, the pieces used in this batch were all 2 yards (measured with the selvedge) long because I like a long scarf! I determined the width by the fold and notch method discussed in chapter 1. The bolt width, when folded and notched to make four equal pieces, produced four scarves that measured approximately 13$\frac{1}{2}$ by 72 inches, each totaling $\frac{1}{2}$ yard of off-bolt fabric. It is important to remove the selvedges before dyeing so that all four edges of the finished piece have the same look.

Step 1: Remove one piece of presoaked wool to a 6-foot work surface. I used Dorr's Marigold wool for this batch.

You can vary the look of this technique by using two colors of dye instead of one.

(as shown here), then fold back this extension at the fold to make a three-section fan pleat, with each section being approximately 2¼ inches wide. Take care to make the folds as equal and neat as possible. Use straight pins to secure.

Step 4: Carefully turn the entire piece over so that the original underneath section is now on top. Fold it in the same way.

Now you have a 2-yard long pleated "fan" in six equal sections. Tweak and adjust the pleats so that they are as smooth and uniform as possible.

Step 5: Starting at one end, tightly roll the pleated wool until the entire length is rolled up into one big coil, like a jelly roll.

Secure the outside end of the wool with a T pin so that it can't unroll.

Step 2: Fold the wool in half along the entire length of the piece. Thus folded, the wool now measures approximately 6¾ by 72 inches.

Step 3: Pick up the top, torn, long edge on the left and bring it back toward the fold, making a fan or accordion pleat. Overshoot the original fold

Step 8: Add the mixed dye to a medium size pot with about $3/4$ inch clear, boiling water. Add $1/2$ tsp. of citric acid or $1/4$ cup of clear vinegar.

Step 6: Prepare a double thickness of natural wool, the folded width of which is slightly narrower than the width of the coil you just made. For example, if the pleated coil is $2 1/4$ inches wide, you will need a folded width that is about $1 3/4$ inches wide. The folds will direct the dye to the creases and prevent the dye from permeating the flat part of the pleat. The length of this natural wool wrap needs to be long enough so it can go around the coil two times, creating a protective sleeve that is four layers thick.

Remove the T pin, and carefully wrap the coil with the natural wool strip, reinserting the T pin at the overlap and adding at least two or three T pins at other places around the circumference of the coil. Use natural or white wool for this wrapping process so that this protective piece cannot bleed any colors into the roll. Once everything is neat and tidy, lay the coil on its flat side and gently press down on the edges of all those folds. If you spot a fold that is too high or too low, adjust to get everything as even as possible. Turn it over, and repeat the final tweaking process.

Step 7: Using a color that will make a good contrast, measure $1/8$ tsp. of dry dye into 1 cup boiling water, stirring well to incorporate. In this example, I used PC #508 Mahogany.

Step 9: Once the mixture has come to a boil, carefully lay one flat side of the rolled wool in the dye pot. If the dye wants to foam aggressively at first, use the tongs to raise the coil so the top is not overwhelmed by the dye bath. Eventually, the foam will calm down.

Step 10: Gently raise the coil every 15 seconds or so to ensure a good distribution of color to the underneath side of the wool. If it only sits flat on the bottom of the pot, it's hard for the dye to soak into all those folded edges on the underneath side. Pick up the entire piece—up and down, up and down—or pry up one edge for a few seconds, then move to a different side and pry up that edge. It does not take much effort to coax the dye under the piece.

Step 11: Cook this first side of the coil until the dye seems to have been well incorporated into the folds of the wool. To check, use the tongs to pick up the piece and look at the bottom side.

This shot shows a coil that is not as dark in the center sections as it is on the outside. It needs to go back in the bath for a few more minutes. Keep raising the wool so that enough dye can get to the bottom coils. It will take a good 8 to 10 minutes of cooking time to get a rich, even color. Cook until the dye water becomes fairly clear.

Step 12: When the first side is dyed in a deep, even color, take the coil out of the pot and set it aside. Mix another $1/8$ tsp. of dye in 1 cup of water and add it back into the original dye bath. Check the water depth to make sure it is about $3/4$ inch deep. Add another bit of citric acid or vinegar. Put the undyed side of the coil into the new bath, and repeat the process until the fold edges have been dyed a deep, rich value.

Step 13: Remove the dyed wool from the bath. Should you ever want striped wool fabric to hook or a striped scarf to wear, proceed to step 20 and follow the directions for finishing the roll. If you are continuing the process, immediately rinse the coil with cold water so the wool becomes cool enough to handle. Remove the pins, and unfold the piece to examine it. (Set the protective sleeve aside.) Even with a tight fold and roll, a few nooks and crannies will have allowed dye seepage. I like a bit of variation. Even so, most of the lines, at this stage, will run the length of the piece.

Jelly Roll 71

Step 14: To form squares, make a second fold at a right angle to the lines from the first folds. To determine the position of this new fold, do a quick measure of the dye lines in the wool. Most of my lines in this example came at intervals of approximately 2¼ inches. Therefore, I established the first new fold at 2¼ inches and then stacked up all the rest of the folds at that interval as evenly as possible. Start at one end and fold or pleat until the entire 2-yard length has been covered.

Step 15: Once all the new folds have been made (27 folds, creating 28 squares), again tweak to get everything as even as possible.

Step 16: Starting at one end, once again roll up the accordion fold in jelly-roll fashion. Since the piece is only about 13 inches long, it will be a little bit harder to roll. Take your time and do a neat job.

 REMOVE THE PINS

While it is fine to use lots of straight pins to keep creases together during the folding and rolling process, be sure to remove the interior straight pins once the roll is secured with the white sleeve and outer T pins, before the actual cooking process begins. Some straight pins will rust and color the fabric.

Step 17: Just like before, have a new double-folded length of natural wool ready that is slightly narrower than the width of your roll. Do a double wrap around the new coil, and secure the edge with a T pin. Insert other T pins at two or three locations around the coil so that everything will stay together securely.

Step 18: Mix up another batch of dye—⅛ tsp. in 1 cup boiling water—and add it to the pot along with a bit of citric acid. Make sure the water depth is no more than ½ to ¾ inch deep.

Step 19: When the dye bath comes to a boil, add the coil and cook it until the folds on the first side have soaked up the dye in an even, dark value. This will take another 10 minutes or so of cooking. Lift and tip the roll periodically to make sure the dye can get to the bottom of the coil and do its work. When the first new side is dyed, remove the coil and add another ⅛ tsp. of mixed dye to the pot and repeat the process with the final undyed side of the coil. When finished, remove the wool and set this dye bath aside. Do not dump it out.

Step 20: The final step can be done in a couple of different ways. To get a finished product with the sharpest markings, put the entire coil, still wrapped as it came out of the last bath, in a pot of clear boiling water and citric acid. Cook the entire piece for 1 hour.

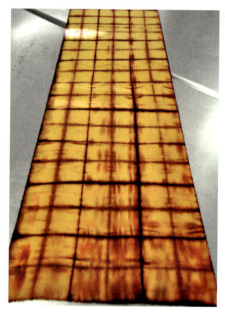

A tightly wrapped coil will keep dye movement to a minimum during the final cooking period. Even so, there will be some interesting coloration that takes place.

If you want a little more bleeding and color movement, unwrap the coil completely and place the wool in a kettle of clear boiling water with citric acid. Once unwrapped, some color will move around in the water before everything starts to set. This technique softens the lines a bit.

When the colors of the folded lines are set, there is nothing stopping you from overdyeing the whole piece with one or two other colors. It would be very easy, for example, to dip the ends in one color and the middle in another before putting the piece in clear water to cook for an hour.

 TIP   **YOU CAN DOWNSIZE**

If the prospect of working on a 72-inch-long piece of wool seems daunting, downsize your project. Square pieces of fabric, 18, 20, or 24 inches can easily be folded, rolled and dyed with this same process to make very interesting pieces that are prefect for quilting, applique, and pillow tops.

My examples have been limited to square and diamond folds, with one to two colors of dye, over solid-colored wool. If you are willing to put in the time and effort, however, there is no limit to the elaborate configurations you can devise.

COOK IT AGAIN

The natural wool protective sleeves, which will also be rather stripy looking at this point because they were folded, might as well be cooked and turned into something useful. Just throw them back in the original dye pot with a bit of citric acid so the white sections of the wool can soak up the remaining color that was not taken by the last coil. Sometimes, after allowing those pieces to cook and soak up most of the dye, I throw the entire scarf in the pink water and let the whole pot cook together for 1 hour to set. If you proceed this way over Marigold, the wool will change to a true orange.

Jelly Roll   73

DYEING WITH COMMERCIAL ACID DYE

batch 8

Your Own Wheel of Color

All dyers need a basic knowledge of what happens to colors when they hook up with other colors. What better way to learn than with a dye project!

Ways to Use a Wheel of Color

- Create a related rainbow stash of wool in your favorite colors
- Raise your level of knowledge of color theory
- Improve your confidence when dyeing without recipes

With just three colors of dye and 27 small pieces of fabric, make this color wheel in nine little batches.

While any of the master batches described in the earlier sections of this book can be made from a special recipe or mixture of two or more dye colors, nearly all of my examples for those sections were dyed with a single measurement of one commercial premixed color. This batch, however, and several that follow, require the mixing or, perhaps more accurately, the mingling of two or more colors.

Winter Bird Tea Cozy, *9½" x 12", #6- and 8-cut wool on primitive linen with appliquéd 3-D embellishments and braided edge. Designed and hooked by Gene Shepherd, Anaheim, California, 2013.*
The blue, red, and green wool used in this piece are all related because they come from a special "Wheel of Color" dye session.

You can, of course, take all the guesswork out of the dyeing with recipes and instruction manuals that provide exact measurements for almost any color you need—as long as you have everything on hand. In fact, I have a drawer full of several wonderful systems that produce a broad range of colors. Even with all those options, I often find myself hunting for that certain elusive color or without the specific dye colors called for in a recipe. Of course, I don't usually notice that I am out of a color until the dye pots are boiling in the middle of a session.

Because we often have to make do with what we have on hand, all dyers need a basic knowledge of what happens to one color when it hooks up with another color. Not only does this help us better understand what we are doing, it also helps us be better, more spontaneous dyers. There is no better way to see all the colors at work than by dyeing a color wheel with the three primary colors: red, yellow, and blue. All other colors are made from a blend of two or more of the primary colors. While color can also be defined in terms of how it reacts to light, for our purposes, white is the absence of all pigment and black contains all three colors—at least, in theory.

Your Own Wheel of Color 75

Version 1: Wheel of Color

This version requires 27 pieces of natural or white presoaked wool fabric in 1/16-yard pieces. Three 1/4 tsp. of dye will be used to create nine different dye pots of color. Since all nine minibatches do not have to be cooked at the same time, you may want to save and store some of the unused dye solutions until you are ready for them. They will keep in a refrigerator in sealed glass containers for up to several weeks.

All the colors in this first version of a color wheel were made with PC #490 Brilliant Blue, PC #338 Magenta, PC #119 Yellow. These colors were chosen because they are pure, strong versions of the primary colors. It is best to have three 4-cup mixing vessels and six 1-cup mixing vessels on hand when making the initial dye recipes. The containers should be arranged in a circle in the order shown here: one large, two small, one large, two small, one large, two small. Although measuring cups are nice for this project, a combination of quart and pint wide-mouth glass jars will also work just fine.

Step 1: In one of the large cups, mix 1/4 tsp. of PC #338 Magenta in 3 cups boiling water, being sure to stir very well so all the dye dissolves. This will produce 3 cups red dye. Using the other large cups, mix up two similar 3-cup batches of dye: one with Brilliant Blue and the other with Yellow. These three will be the master colors for this batch and should be arranged as shown in the ring with the smaller vessels.

Step 2: Starting with whichever master color you wish (red is shown here), remove 2/3 cup of color from the master vessel to each of the adjacent cups on its immediate right and left. To the second cup over, on both the right and left of the master vessel, add 1/3 cup of color. I have more control of my dye by dipping, so I use a 1/3 measuring cup to transfer the color.

That first step will have produced five measuring cups that now have some red dye. Because two-thirds of the liquid has been removed to the cups on either side of the master vessel, the master vessel will now contain just 1 cup of red color.

Step 3: Repeat step 2 with both the yellow and the blue master cups. This means that 2/3 cup of yellow will be transferred to the closest cup on each side of the yellow master vessel. In this case, 2/3 cup of yellow will go in the measuring cup that already contains 1/3 cup of red. The cup just next to it will receive the addition of 1/3 cup of yellow to the waiting 2/3 cup of red. When all three master vessels have been distributed in this way, there will be three vessels of pure color and six cups of mixed colors. Each will contain just 1 cup of liquid.

Once all nine color solutions have been mixed, they can be kept or stored until each is ready to go in a dye pot. Since I have nine smaller pots and the ability to cook them all at once, I usually go straight into a dyeing session. However, if you only have one or two pots, dye them up one or two at a time.

Step 4: Dye three 1/16-yard pieces of fabric in each of the nine separate colors. For this wheel of color, I used a modified Lazy Swatch technique (as described in batch 4). Because it is such a small amount of wool, however, a 4-quart pot half full of water is adequate. Remember to add both the dye mixture and 1/2 tsp. of citric acid before the staggered addition of the three wool pieces to the simmering water. As with all applications described in the book, cook time is 1 hour after the last piece of wool is added.

> **TIP** **TEXTURES AND WHITES**
>
> When presoaking a mixture of textured and natural/white wool, keep the textures soaking in a separate container so that none of the color can contaminate the natural wool before dyeing. I even separate black textures from brown textures when soaking.

Primary Dipping Made Visual

If all that dipping seems a little daunting, here is a visual that will help you remember how to distribute the dye from the three original 3-cup master solutions of this batch.

Primary Red = 3 parts Red
- Mixed Red Orange = 2 parts Red and 1 part Yellow
- Mixed Orange = 1 part Red and 2 parts Yellow

Primary Yellow = 3 parts Yellow
- Mixed Yellow Green = 2 parts Yellow and 1 part Blue
- Mixed Blue Green = 1 part Yellow and 2 parts Blue

Primary Blue = 3 parts Blue
- Mixed Violet = 2 parts Blue and 1 part Red
- Mixed Purple = 1 part Blue and 2 parts Red

The parts, once distributed amongst the nine cups, are represented in this photo by primary colored squares of paper. The three primary colors—red, yellow, and blue—each retain 3 parts and then also pass on 3 parts to each immediate side of the wheel.

RESULT: PC #490 BRILLIANT BLUE, #338 MAGENTA, AND #119 YELLOW OVER NATURAL WOOL

> **TIP — HOT HANDLES**
>
> When the metal handle on the dipper gets too hot to hold, a pair of pliers doubles as a non-heat-sensitive gripping device!

While this process helps us easily understand the way the primary colors work together to produce the wonderful mixed-color byproducts that we love, it also produces a multivalued stash just waiting for your next project. However, should you not want quite as much variation, you can tweak this procedure to your particular liking.

If you don't want to produce three values in each pot, adapt the procedure. Instead of adding three pieces of wool, put in 1½ to 2 pieces all at once. The smaller amounts of wool will soak up more dye and produce a darker value. If you want the lightest value of color, either decrease the amount of dye or increase the number of wool pieces to five or six. With more wool, there will be less dye to go around, resulting in lighter values. (Of course, more wool will also require a bigger pot and more clear water in the bath.) Three pieces of wool put in at the same time would produce three pieces of the medium value. An artist who likes to use traditional multivalue swatches could even take the original cup of mixed dye and use it as the base for a traditional multivalue swatch as discussed in batch 5.

Version 2: Personal Wheel of Color

If the colors in the first example are a little strong for you, here is a second version tailored specifically for you.

Version 2 should be done exactly like the first wheel with two exceptions:

- Pick any red, yellow, and blue that you like. These should be your favorites.
- Decrease the amount of dye used to make the three master colors; use ⅛ tsp. of each color instead of ¼ tsp.

For this Personal Wheel of Color, I stayed away from pure colors and went with blends that I particularly like. PC #122 Mustard, for example, has a little red in it, and PC #508 Mahogany has a little blue. The third color was PC #440 Bright Blue. I like all three of these colors and use them all the time. Therefore, if I put these three together, I can expect the end result will be pleasing to my eye. After all, so much in color selection ends up being about what resonates with the eye of the artist. Therefore, build this second batch on colors you like.

Once you have chosen three new colors, follow all the steps from version 1 to make a personalized wheel.

Since half the amount of dye was used for the personalized wheel, the resulting fabric has much lighter values. There is something particularly pleasing about this combination of wool. All the resultant pieces are related and go together because of their shared parentage. With this bundle of dyed wool in my personal stash, I know that there will be plenty of color options ready and waiting for my next project.

RESULT: PC #122 MUSTARD, #440 BRIGHT BLUE, AND #508 MAHOGANY OVER NATURAL WOOL

> **TIP — EXTRA STIRRING**
>
> Extra dye in the master measuring cups requires extra stirring before you can divide the dye mixtures among the other jars. Larger amounts of wool, of course, will also require a bigger dye pot.

Version 3: Downsizing a Wheel with Glass Jars

If lack of equipment keeps you from trying this technique, you can easily adapt the process to dye eighteen 1/16-yard pieces of wool in nine glass pint jars of any kind or shape.

I mixed 1/16 tsp. each of PC #440 Bright Blue, PC #122 Mustard, and PC #508 Mahogany for this batch. (Because I was dyeing less wool in a small space, I cut the amount of dye in half once again from what I used in version 2.) Mix the dyes in the initial 3-cup containers and distribute them among the nine jars as described earlier.

Once all the pint jars have received their proper amounts of dye, add $1/2$ tsp. of citric acid or a little white vinegar to each jar. Then add a $1/16$-yard piece of wool to each jar. To ensure that there are no white spots in the finished product, use a utensil to plunge the wool fabric up and down a couple times before pushing it under the surface of the bath.

Place the jars of wool on a wire rack in a bath of simmering water. To ensure that the jars do not tip over, use leftover aluminum foil to stabilize them.

Immediately insert a second $1/16$-yard piece of wool in each jar, taking extra care to make sure that the wool gets good exposure to the dye bath. Add enough extra boiling water to each jar to cover the wool. Once the jars are

mixed and full of water, push the wool down enough to ensure that it will stay under the surface of the bath as it cooks.

Add additional water to the host pan so the level of water comes up to the neck of the jar. When the host bath is simmering, cover the pan with a lid and cook for 1 hour to set the wool. Check every so often to make sure the water levels both inside and outside the jars are sufficient.

Scrunching the wool tightly in such a small space produces a distinctive look. To make values of color that are closer together than those in this example, add the second piece of wool sooner. If you only want nine pieces of wool, instead of the 18 pieces shown, decrease the amount of dye from $1/16$ to $1/32$ tsp. This method creates a lot of options for your artistic palette.

It's a Small World . . .

Yes, you can adapt! When it came time to whip the edge of my little nylon rug, *Carnival Paws*, shown in batch 15, I adapted the Wheel of Color method in order to produce an even bigger rainbow selection of wool yarn. Since each hank only contained about 4 yards of natural yarn, I made miniscule amounts of the master dyes, from which I could spoon out enough to create this batch. Still, I followed the same basic principles as described in this section: nine little batches of dye, some with staggered additions of multiple hanks. As with all dyeing, but even more so with these tiny batches, it is important to let your eye call some of the shots.

. . . Or a Supersized World

This supersized version of the Wheel of Color produced 9 yards of dyed wool fabric.

To supersize a batch, just add extra dye to the original three 3-cup master vessels. In this case, I increased the original amount of dye to 1 tsp. for each of the master colors so I could dye four ¼ yards of fabric in each color of the wheel. Although the mixing process will stay the same, increased dye concentration will make it possible to dye more wool in each of nine colors. As before, use any combination of red, yellow, and blue; I chose 1 tsp. each of PC #508 Mahogany, PC #122 Mustard, and PC #440 Bright Blue.

Creating a big stash of multivalue solids and textures in a wheel of colors that you like gives you a ready supply of wool for those times when you need just a little bit of this and that to make a project pop. Quarter-yard pieces of three solids and one texture were overdyed for each of the nine colors.

DYEING WITH COMMERCIAL ACID DYE

batch 9

Spot Dyes

Spot dyes are full of surprises.

▲▲▲
When cut and hooked, spotted wool brings an immediate sparkle, glow, or shine to whatever it accentuates.
▲▲▲

Although it is possible to get both value and color variations in a single recipe dye bath with the previous techniques, both value and coloration can be much more aggressively controlled with a spot dye process.

Consider these basic spot dye guidelines *before* you attempt any spot dye technique.

Water: Since water is a conduit for all mixed dye, a pan with lots of water provides dye with lots of opportunity for movement to other places in the pan. If multiple dyes move in a lot of water, they will mingle—a lot. A pan with limited water restricts the movement of dye, helping to keep the spots of color separated. Although some mingling always takes place, less water will keep color spots distinct and recognizable; more water will produce much greater changes in the coloration.

Surface Area: In this method, spots of color are poured on the surface of the wool as it cooks in the pot or pan. Pots, which hold the fiber in a vertical arrangement, provide less surface area than casserole pans. Casserole pans allow the wool to stretch out and present more surface area during the dye process, allowing color to be distributed in a much more systematic way. Additionally, pans allow you to place fabric in right side up, ensuring that, when finished, the spots of color will end up on the side where they are desired. (See the sidebar on page 87.) I usually do spot dyes in casserole pans.

Basic Color Theory: Never forget that there are three primary colors: red, yellow, and blue. All others colors are made from a blend of two or more of the primary colors. When all the primary colors, in pure form or as part of another color, are mingled to make one new color, the usual result is gray or muddy brown. For that reason, our goal is to limit the movement of most colors.

Ways to Use Spot Dyes

- Outlines and fill that sparkle with color variation
- Hooked and prodded vegetation, leaves, fruit, and flowers
- Wool for hooking animals
- Backgrounds

Harbor Lights, *9" x 12", #5-, 6-, and 8-cut wool on linen. Designed and hooked by Laura Pierce, Petaluma, California, 2012. The sunset reflections of dark magenta and pale purple are all spot dyes made with leftover dye solutions the artist had saved from previous sessions. In this instance, she spotted over Dorr's pink wool.* Photo by Laura Pierce

As an illustration of how the primary colors work, I spotted red, yellow, and blue dyes on three distinct outside sections of this piece of natural wool fabric. Each color was encouraged to move out into the no man's land between the big spots and interact with its immediate neighbors. When the red and yellow got together, a reddish orange resulted. Yellow and blue made greens, while blue and red made purples. As very little host water and dye were used in this process, interaction was basically limited to two colors at a time.

Once the wool piece was dyed, however, I dumped the remaining red, yellow, and blue dye mixtures into one pot of water so that they could mix completely and added another piece of wool. In this case, all that mingling produced gray. Unless you want sections in the spot dye with grays or muddy browns, take care with the amount of color you place in the pan.

Agitation and Setting Time:
Agitation of wool during the spotting process, particularly before the colors are set, mingles the colors. Just as a child's marble will roll down an inclined board, dye will move down wool that is picked up, repositioned, or stirred before the colors are set. Such agitation moves color from the place where it is desired into the bath, where those wild color parties may produce dull hangover colors. This fact calls for patience, a virtue I have not been blessed with. Because of the lessons taught in the school of hard knocks, I can attest that spots need to be left alone for a while so they can set. To facilitate that process, I usually add citric acid to either the initial bath water or to each dye.

Version 1: One-Color-Family Spot

RESULT: PC #304 CAPE COD CRANBERRY, #306 TURKEY RED, #351 BRIGHT RED, #366 RED, AND #338 MAGENTA OVER NATURAL WOOL

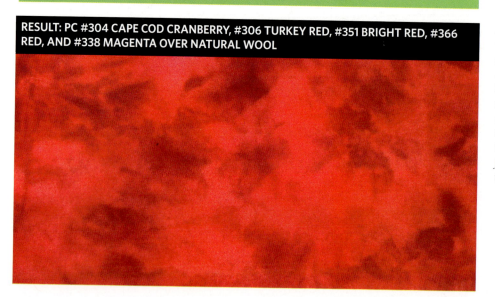

A one-color-family spot provides a good vehicle for experimentation with the basic spot guidelines. Although I call it KFC Red and suggest that it is created from a blend of 11 different herbs and spices, this spot technique really isn't all that complicated. This version uses five different colors of red, and it could just as easily be done with five different selections from another color family. This technique is particularly good for backgrounds.

Rebellious Reds

Even with lots of stirring and boiling water, red dyes often end up clotting. Control this by adding some Glauber salt to the measuring cup while the initial mixture is being prepared. If no Glauber salt is available, a squirt of Jet Dry can be substituted to help get a more complete mixture. In my studio, reds are often rebellious even with those additions. I do the best mix I can and then boldly press on.

Step 1: Prep and soak 1 yard of natural wool cut into four pieces.

Step 2: Assemble five different colors from the color family of your choice. My version uses PC #304 Cape Cod Cranberry, PC #306 Turkey Red, PC #351 Bright Red, PC #366 Red, and PC #338 Magenta. This assortment contains reds that would be classified as "maroon," "fire engine," and "rosy."

Step 3: Measure and mix the first four colors each in a separate measuring cup, ¼ tsp. of dye to 1½ cups boiling water. In a fifth cup, dissolve a decidedly heaping ⅜ tsp. #338 Magenta. Set all cups aside.

Step 4: Arrange 1 yard of wool fabric in a large steamer pan with the top side up. Obviously, there will be peaks and valleys in the lie of the wool. Add 1 to 1½ inches water and either citric acid or white vinegar, then turn on the heat until the water starts to boil.

Step 5: Using the darkest color first (#304 in this instance) pour six spots of color in as many valleys of the wool, using all of your mixed dyes. The spots should be distributed equally across the pan. Let the spots of color cook unmolested for 1 to 2 minutes. Take your time and don't hurry the process. However, as the color of the water starts to noticeably get lighter in those spots, use a spoon or tongs to punch

down additional peaks so they too can receive some of that dye. Let the pan cook for a few minutes more before proceeding to the next step. If you want clearly delineated spots, wait until the bath color has gone clear before proceeding. If you want less delineation, proceed when the water is still pink.

Step 6: Using a spoon or tongs, nudge open six more little untouched valleys and add six spots of a second color (#306 in this example) as described in step 5.

Step 7: After the water has cleared from the second application, use a pair of tongs to slightly readjust the wool to bring white, untouched sections of the wool to the surface.

Step 8: Add the third and fourth colors (#351 and #366) in exactly the same way. Although most of the wool should be covered by this time, don't be alarmed if there are still a few spots of fairly white or barely altered fabric.

Spot Dyes 85

Step 9: Up to this point, the water in the pan remains at about the 1 1/2- inch level. Even though four successive 1 1/2 cups of dye solution have been added, constant boiling will have kept the level from rising much. If you want a stronger delineation between the colors, leave the water level as it is and proceed to the final color. However, with this particular set of colors, I prefer to smooth out the differences a bit; do this by adding another couple of inches of clear water to the pan.

Step 10 (top right): For the last step, take your mixture of 3/8 tsp. of PC #338 Magenta in 1 1/2 cups boiling water. Stir it, pour it in a 2-quart saucepan, and fill the pan with water. Using this saucepan of dye solution, once again spot in about six locations in the steamer pan. Given the increased volume of both clear and colored water, the new color will be most efficient in moving about the pan. In effect, this last color will create an uneven wash that will unite everything. If you want strong delineation between the colors, do not add any more water to the pan or to the #338 after its initial mix.

Once the last dye has been added, reduce heat to a simmer and cover the wool with a lid. Cook the wool at this temperature for 1 hour.

In the Pink

It is always a good idea to multitask by including a bit of yarn in your dye pan or pot, and you don't have to always use white or natural-colored yarn. When making this batch of KFC Red, I added some pink yarn to both the soak and the dye pan.

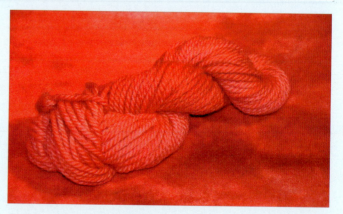

Coming from the right family, the pink yarn was ready, willing, and able to amp up its profile with some much hotter KFC family values.

86 Prepared to Dye

Which Side is the Right Side?

The edge of this fabric was created when the selvedge was torn and removed. If I were running this wool through the cutter, in the normal way, it would be cut in the direction, bottom to top, of that torn edge. The larger exposed section of the wool, on the right, shows the top, or right, side of the wool. Careful inspection will show that the threads seem to have a vertical look about them; they lie running up and down like the warp threads of the fabric. The threads on the smaller section of fabric (left side) seem to lie running in a more horizontal or sideways fashion; that is the back side. When strips of wool are cut, those looks are even more pronounced. To hook "using the right side" means pulling the loops so that the right side of the fabric is the top side of the loop—the side that shows on the loop. If you are always going to check and pull your loops so that the top side of the fabric shows, then make sure your spotted fabric is dyed so that the main bursts of color sit on that side.

The right side of the wool is the *warp face* of the fabric—the top side. To see the difference between right and wrong, or top side and bottom, turn over the edge of any fabric so the back and front can be seen at one time.

What Difference Does Right and Wrong Make?

As far as rug durability is concerned, either side is fine. The issue is one of aesthetics.

- **Loops pulled from strips to show the right side of the wool** tend to look smoother because the majority of visible threads run the length of those strips. Consequently, I think they have a bit more shine or finished quality about them.

- **Loops pulled showing the wrong side,** because the threads tend to show in the opposite (side to side) direction, look a little choppy or rough. I think they look a little flat in how they catch the light.

- There is nothing at stake, structurally, when choosing sides. Each version makes a well-constructed rug.

- Some artists cut strips and make rugs for decades never bothering to check which side is right and which side is wrong. They argue, and rightly so, that there is some value to taking the strips as they come out of the cut pile. Such variety causes the loops of the piece to catch the light in different ways, thereby making the look of the rug more interesting. Many people (and I am one) hooked two or three rugs never even knowing there was a right or wrong side. I can't say that my satisfaction level with those rugs lessened after learning about right side vs. wrong side.

- I normally look at each strip before I hook and use the right side as the top side for my loops. I like the look that the right side creates. Now that I know and look for it, I think I can tell a slight difference. I do, on occasion, exploit those differences. Sometimes I even use the right side of the wool when hooking a shiny section of a flower and the wrong side when putting in a shadow next to it. When dyeing wool that has a one-sided application (like most casserole dyes), I attempt to put the dyes directly on the top side of the wool. This requires me to check each piece of wool before it is put into a casserole pan so I can make sure that it is lying right side up.

- If you don't care about the subtle nuances of each side, then hook on, consistently, never paying attention! So much in hooking is about being consistent. If you want to change your style, then don't change in the middle of a piece.

- Final confession: when faced with a piece of wool that has all the beautiful coloration I like on its back side, I use the back side.

Spot Dyes 87

Version 2: Transitional Spot

On those occasions when a color bridge is needed to go between two distinctly different colors of spotted wool, make your own transitional spot. A batch of Peace Rose in Three Pans is a perfect example of a transitional spot.

Although my version was designed specifically for a prodded peace rose, the same principle can be applied to any two colors that need to be united.

Step 2: Put 2 inches of water and a bit of citric acid in three casserole pans. Place one piece of wool in each pan, and turn on the heat.

Step 3: Begin spotting with teaspoons of the Buttercup Yellow. Pick a valley in the wool to test the strength of the first teaspoon. Submerse the spoon with a little swish. Because this wool needs to be a very pale yellow with limited hotter yellow highlights, diluting 1 tsp. of dye this way keeps the color soft. Hotter spots of yellow can be added by spotting on the peaks of the wool sticking out of the water. If a peak appears to be too hot, use the spoon to push the offending spot under the water, where it will be diluted.

Step 1: Choose two colors of dye. I used Cushing's Cherry and Buttercup Yellow. As it takes very little dye for this particular process, only mix up a small amount of each; $1/32$ tsp. to 1 cup of boiling water is more than enough for three $1/4$-yard pieces of wool.

The finished product should have some delicate highs and lows of the color.

Step 4: In the same fashion, spot the Cherry in one of the other pans. Colors always look darker when wet, but even so, it is very easy to get carried away. Think *delicate* peace rose while spotting and keep things light.

Step 5: In the middle pan, make some spots with Cherry and then make some spots with Buttercup Yellow.

The goal is to make wool with separate blushes of yellow and pink (as you can see below, left), so keep the water level low and the spots far enough apart that they don't really mix. It is even fine to have a little natural wool showing on this step. Too much dye in too close a proximity will create orange wool, not the delicate, blushing wool of the Peace rose. Take your time. While you can always add a little more dye, it is really hard to remove it! When each of the three pans has been spotted to your satisfaction, cover each with a lid and cook for 1 hour to set.

RESULT: CUSHING'S CHERRY AND BUTTERCUP YELLOW, SEPARATE AND TOGETHER, OVER NATURAL WOOL

When spots from two different pure colors intermingle, the resultant dyed wool will be a new transitional color. This new special spot can either stand alone or, as in the case of the Peace rose trio, be used to make a transition between the two parent colors.

Transitional spot pieces can also be made in a single pan as long as you remember that there will be a little extra surprise movement of color. In this particular detailed shot, yellow spots from four different colors of dye were made across the center section of this piece. A few blue spots intermingled with the yellow, creating a greenish-blue section, and reds intermingled, making apricot/coral spots.

Spot Dyes

Multiple Unions in One Pan

Step 1: Since three color family groups take a bit more room, use a 1/2-yard piece of wool (18 by 56 inches) for this process. After soaking, place the fabric right side up in a steamer pan with 1 inch of water and bring it to a boil. Add citric acid at this time.

Step 2: Although any combination of color families can be mingled in this way, this example uses the three primary colors: yellow, blue, and red. Each color family used four different dyes. I chose four yellows (PC #119, #122, #123, and #228), four blues (PC #407, #411, #440, and #490) and four reds (PC #304, #306, #338, and #351). Any combination of four will work, although combinations that exhibit some noticeable differences produce more noticeable spots. Each dye was mixed in a separate container: 1/32 tsp. dye to 3/4 cup boiling water.

How Do I Use a Piece of Wool Like This?

Many people look at a piece of wool with multiple unions like this and think: *It is beautiful but . . . how could I possibly use it?* While I understand this particular rainbow of options might present a challenge for a single project, who made the rule that says one has to use a large piece in a single project?

- ▲ Cut it into four or five different sections, reserving each one for an appropriate project. Perhaps one section looks made for leaves while another is perfect for flowers.
- ▲ Run the entire piece through your cutter and keep it on hand for strips that add pop—hooked sections or lines that need a little bit of color or highlights. You could actually cut the wool in either direction. Short cuts (with the selvedge) will keep sections of spotted color together. A long cut across the entire width of the fabric will produce single strips with all the colors. Such rainbow strips are effective as outline wool for outline-and-fill projects.
- ▲ You do not have to make your wool with these colors. Pick the family groups you like or need for any given project and make your own unique pan. For example: If you need green and orange foliage for a fall project, make a section of green spots and section of orange spots, and then mingle the two in the middle. Should both red and brown be needed in such a fall project, make a multiple union pan that substitutes these colors: browns, space, greens, space, oranges, space, reds, and so on. The combinations are limitless, and the technique can be most helpful to any project where colors can use some help making transitions.

Step 3: Make separate spotted zones with the basic color family groups, skipping a space of natural wool before making a new section of spots. In this piece, the coloration at this stage was (from the left) yellow, natural space, blue, natural space, red, natural space, yellow. Although each color grouping is not in a separate pan, each color grouping should be separated by a space of undyed wool.

Step 4: In the undyed spaces, make alternate spots of the two closest family groups to be joined. Pick one color and make several spots in the no man's land of natural wool. Follow it with one color from the other side. So, if joining yellow and blue, do one blue and then one yellow, followed by a second blue and a second yellow, and so on. This is not an exact science. Spot away to your heart's content until you like what you see. You do not have to use all of the dye or even equal amounts of the colors. If a color runs low, make a little more. If a color seems too strong and cannot be diluted by swishing it in the water as you spot, then dilute the color with a little water before making more spots.

An 18-inch by bolt-long piece of wool provides enough space to mingle multiple colors. The technique is pretty much the same as that used to unify the two colors in the Peace rose wool, but this single-pan batch mingled at least three families of colors.

Version 3: Lotsaspots

If one or two color families can be delicately mixed to create useful pieces of wool fabric, then a lot more colors can boldly band together in one steam pan to do the same thing. In light of what we have already discussed, look at this piece of finished fabric and ask yourself: *How was this wool made?* If you thought, *Stronger dye, more colors, shallow water, and little agitation,* you were right.

Step 1: Pick five or six colors that you think go well together. The photo at right shows a piece of wool that was made with PC #508 Mahogany, PC #808 Raspberry, PC #819 Purple, PC #123 Toffee, PC #135 Yellow, and PC #338 Magenta.

If you are having trouble finding the right combination of colors to spot, analyze a visual. What colors, for instance, show up in the coloration and shadows of that brick wall you are trying to depict? If it is a combination of various reds, browns, and a little purple, then pick from those colors.

Step 2: Starting with the darkest color, use teaspoons of color to make some random spots throughout the pan.

Step 3: Allow the dye to set awhile before adding a second color. Add the second color.

It Does Not Take Too Much To Be Related

To save time, I often do two different pieces in the same pan. What makes a setup like this work is the fact that two of the colors (the yellow spots) were used across both pieces. The pan is a two-yellow spot dye over all the wool, with extra red and purple highlights on one end and extra blue and purple highlights on the other. The pieces, while different, can get along together in the pot because they are related.

92   Prepared to Dye

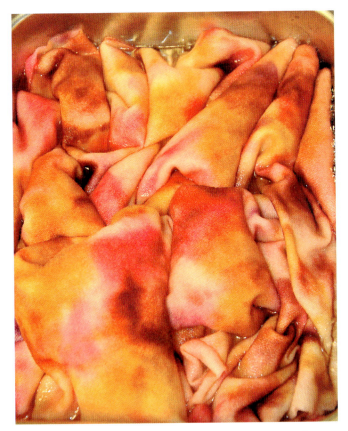

Step 4: Allow the second color time to set, reposition the wool in the pan, and re-spot with the first two colors, and then add a third. Continue in that fashion—spotting, resting, spotting, repositioning—until the wool reaches the desired appearance. Limited agitation preserves the spotty appearance; more agitation lessens it.

Don't forget: any spot-dying process lends itself to double duty. You can easily spot dye both wool fabric and wool yarn at the same time.

Selecting Colors

What colors should be used together? The right answer is, of course, the colors you want to use. You can mix just about anything together as long as you follow a few basic rules:

Don't overdo it. Too many colors can create an unsalvageable situation that ends up a muddy mess.

Always remember how colors blend to make other colors. If you don't want to end up with browns or grays, then don't spot large amounts of the primary colors in close proximity to each other.

Take your time. Even with the early addition of citric acid and heat, dye takes time to set. Think of colors as having short attention spans. They hit the bath ready to party, and if they find other colors, the party takes off. However, if there are no other colors there to party with, the colors will turn their focus to setting. Wait for each color to be well committed to setting before adding the next. Some changing will still take place, but it will be in a much more subdued manner.

RESULT: PC #508 MAHOGANY, #808 RASPBERRY, #819 PURPLE, #123 TOFFEE, #135 YELLOW, #338 MAGENTA, AND #733 IVY OVER NATURAL WOOL

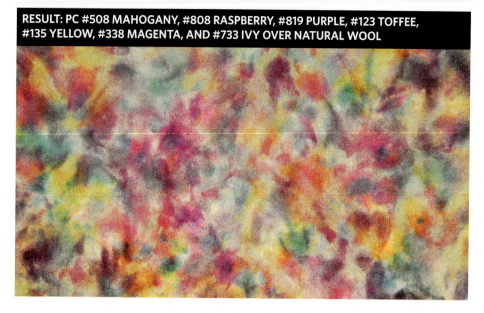

A quick look might make you think this is a totally new spot dye combination. However, it was made with exactly the same dyes as those used in the initial Lotsaspots at the beginning of this section, with one addition: PC #733 Ivy.

RESULT: PC #507 MAHOGANY, #808 RASPBERRY, #819 PURPLE, AND #411 PERIWINKLE OVER NATURAL WOOL

This rosy Lotsaspots started out with half of the original colors from the previous example: PC #508 Mahogany, PC #808 Raspberry, and PC #819 Purple. Even with the addition of one new color, PC #411 Periwinkle, the resultant wool is nicely related to the other two pieces.

RESULT: PC #508 MAHOGANY, #808 RASPBERRY, #819 PURPLE, AND #733 IVY OVER NATURAL WOOL

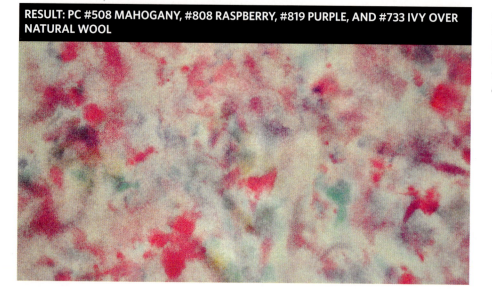

Once again, PC #508 Mahogany, PC #808 Raspberry, and PC #819 Purple were used to spot this example. However, in this case, I diluted the strength of each dye mixture with water before spotting. I also added a few spots of weak PC #733 Ivy.

Magic Refrigerator Dye

Whenever I have leftover mixed dye, each separate color goes in its own pint jar and is covered with a lid and ring. The jars then go in a little dedicated fridge that sits under my dye sink where they can be kept for several weeks. Refrigeration is important as mixed dyes stored at room temperature will eventually mold. When all the shelves are full of jars, it is time for a Magic Refrigerator Dye Day.

Even though the colors coming out of the refrigerator vary from session to session, I always end up with wool that is stunning. That is due, quite simply, to my secret magic dye ingredient.

Using a casserole pan holding three or four $1/4$-yard pieces of soaked wool, I spot all the various colors from the refrigerator on the wool, as described in other methods, starting with the darker colors first. I am careful to balance the spots of each color across the wool, as well as give each color time to set before others are added. I do not, however, make any effort to cover up all of the natural wool. Once the final color has begun to clear from the water, I remove the wool to a saucepan. The original casserole pan receives a little more water and the secret magic weapon: $1/2$ tsp. mixed PC #122 Mustard. I then return the wool to the casserole pan and cook for 1 hour. The Mustard creates a wash that works its magic over all the previous spots. While the results certainly vary, I always get wool that is magic!

Version 4: Spots in a Pot

The spot versions shown so far in this batch were all made in a casserole pan. Large flat pans provide more surface area to spot, requiring less rearrangement of fabric or yarn during the spotting process. Spotting in a pot of water usually produces spots that are much bigger and more diffused—like painting with a bigger brush stroke. This method provides yet another option for making spotted wool.

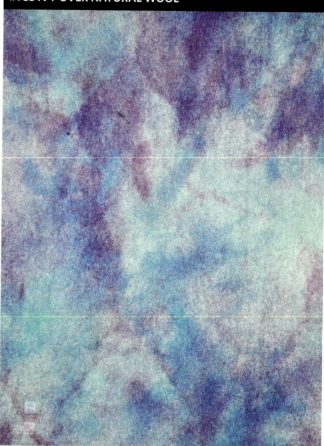

Step 1: Prep four 1/4-yard pieces of wool and place them in a pot. For this method, I prefer pieces that are cut at 18 inches on the selvedge because they are easier to stir. Bring the pot of water to a boil, and add the citric acid.

Step 2: Mix the dyes you wish to use. I used 1/8 tsp. each of PC #490 Brilliant Blue, PC #826 Deep Orchid, and PC #733 Ivy, mixed separately in 1 cup boiling water.

I like the soft look of wool that is spotted in a pot. Although this piece has decided color variations, those changes are not nearly as pronounced as with other methods. These spots are more like strong blushes rather than strong contrasting color jolts.

Step 3: Using the darkest dye (Brillant Blue), partially spot the exposed surface of the wool. Let the dye set for a minute, then gently push the peaks of the wool under the water to help dissipate the dye. Let the wool cook 2 to 3 minutes more until it is obvious that the water is starting to clear.

Step 4: Reposition the wool so that under layers that had little exposure to the first spotting can now come to the surface. Once repositioned in this way, spot again with Brillant Blue as before.

Step 5: After repositioning the wool, make a few spots with the Deep Orchid. As before, let it cook a bit, then push the peaks below the water. Repeat once again with this color as described in the previous step.

If you are patient, you can add any number of dye colors to a pot. However, if you get in a hurry, adding color after color without any pause, you will end up with a muddy bath.

Step 6: After spotting twice each with Blue and Orchid, follow the same slow procedure to spot with the Ivy. Once all three colors have been added, continue to reposition and spot with whichever colors are needed. As these additional spots are made, reposition the wool frequently to make sure there are no white spots left on the wool.

RESULT: PC #490 BRILLIANT BLUE, PC #826 DEEP ORCHID, AND PC #733 IVY OVER NATURAL WOOL

With multiple pieces stacked up vertically in one pot, there can be a lot of variations among finished pieces. However, there's nothing wrong with variation.

TIP — CONTROLLING THE SPOTS

If you need dark spots of dye, pour or spoon the dye as it comes from the measuring cup right on the area of wool you wish to darken. If you need lesser amounts of color in a specific area, push the area under the water with a pair of tongs before adding more dye. As the dye goes into the unoccupied water at that spot, give a little swish with the tongs to mix the strong dye and the excess water. The dye will lighten up before coming in contact with the wool. If a little more color is still needed, do it again. You are in control, so make the wool and dye obey your every wish.

Spots to Suit Your Every Need

Because of the highly controlled effects that can be achieved with spot dyes, each version can be used and adapted to create very special wool to suit the artist's special needs. When contemplating my wool options for an ear of Indian corn, I quickly decided to create a spot dye to make the process as easy as possible.

I make my Indian corn wool in pieces that are the entire width of a bolt of wool. As no pan is big enough to hold a flat piece of wool that size, I lay the entire piece of soaked wool on a large piece of aluminum foil. Using whatever colors I want (mixed with water and vinegar), I randomly spot the wool. Before encasing the wool with a top layer of foil, I carefully add more white vinegar on the long side of the wool. (**Note:** Pouring any liquid directly on top of a spot dye will dissipate the color.) I then seal the top and bottom pieces of foil at the edge with a triple fold. As a foil package this size is too big for a normal oven, the right and left sides should be folded in to make a three-layer, oven-sized packet. Once folded, I place the delicate package in a pan and bake it in the oven at 300° for 1 hour.

By spotting white wool with random drops of red, blue, purple, and yellow, I created a wool that could simply be cut and hooked as is. The highly specific spots did all the work once the hooking began.

98 Prepared to Dye

Dump Dyes

DYEING WITH COMMERCIAL ACID DYE

batch 10

▲▲▲

A dump dye is just that: simply dump in the dye to create a gradation that hooks up very much like a piece of dip-dyed wool.

▲▲▲

Ways to Use Dump Dyes

- Scrolls
- Leaves
- Flowers
- Background
- Any motif that requires a gradation of color or value
- Appliqué

While all wool looks great hanging in my backyard, even I have to admit that a line of yard-long dump-dyed pieces makes a big impact. All of these pieces were dyed using the method in version 2 on page 102.

This method controls color value by the amount of dye mixture that is strategically dumped on the wool as it lies in a large pan. In a dip dye, it is hard to know exactly how long each section of the wool needs to be exposed to the bath in order to get that graduated look. The dump dye method not only takes the guesswork out of the equation, it makes it possible to provide for both gradation and multi-color blending in one process. Although the end result may not have quite as smooth a transition as a traditional dip dye, the resultant mottled look has its own charm. Here are three variations on this technique.

Blown Away, 12½" x 34", wool and cotton appliqué on dump-dyed wool fabric, with embroidery, silk ribbon, and quilted embellishments. Designed and made by Karen Cunagin, Fallbrook, California, 2012. (Background wool dyed by Gene Shepherd.)

If you think your wool is too pretty to cut up, follow Karen's lead and use it as the centerpiece of a stunning quilted display.

Version 1: Single Color Dump Dye in Three Values

RESULT: PC #121 MAPLE SUGAR OVER NATURAL WOOL

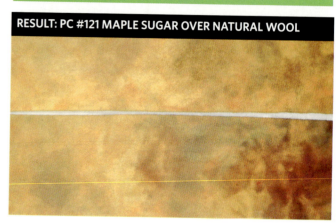

Version 1 produces a single color gradation that is similar to a dip dye. When long pieces of wool have to accept dye in cramped quarters, the end result has more mottling than traditional dip dyes. In most cases, however, I prefer my pieces of wool to have this variation. Pragmatically, the technique is not nearly so fussy as a dip dye.

Step 1: Prep two ¼-yard pieces of natural wool, cut on the selvedge at 36 inches by approximately 13½ inches. Presoak the wool.

Step 2: Prepare three separate mixtures of the same color of dye. For this pan, PC #121 Maple Sugar was used in ¼, ⅛, and 1/16 tsp. amounts. Each was mixed in its own cup with 2 cups boiling water.

Step 3: Make a rough accordion fold along the narrow edge of each presoaked piece. This fold is not intended to be precise; it's just a helpful way to evenly distribute the wool in the pan.

Place the pieces of wool side by side in a large steamer pan. Take special care to evenly scrunch both the width and length of each piece so it uniformly fills up the pan. If you differentiate between the top and bottom side of the wool when hooking your strips, make sure that both pieces lie top side up. Add about 2 to 3 inches of water to the pan, and turn on the heat.

Step 4: When the pan of wool starts to simmer, carefully pour the darkest value (1/4 tsp.) of dye mixture along one end of the wool pieces. Pour in such a way as to encourage the dye to stay on that end of the pan. You may need to delicately use your tongs to nudge the dye along the side of the pan to ensure a uniformly dark edge. After the first dye mixture seems properly organized, pour the medium value of dye (1/8 tsp.) side to side in the middle of the pan. Again, try to keep this medium dye solution in the middle of the pan. Once settled, pour the lightest mixture of dye (1/16 tsp.) on the edge of the wool that is un-dyed. These three mixtures should be poured in as quickly as possible in succession.

Step 5: Use a potato masher or pair of tongs to push the peaks of wool down into the bath. This is particularly important at those intersections where the three different strengths of dye will mingle with each other to lessen the abrupt change in dye strength. Be gentle at this point. The goal is to encourage mingling, not stir the entire pot so that the values are lost. If citric acid is going in late, add it now. By this stage, you should see a gradation that looks similar to this pan of wool (above). If a section is not dark enough, you can always go back and add a little more dye. Normally, if I add any extra dye, it is a little more strong dye at the darkest edge as that end always seems to get cheated.

Step 6: Cover the pan with a lid, lower the heat, and simmer the wool for 1 hour. Check every so often to make sure there is enough water in the pan to keep the wool from scorching.

TIP — TRY THREE

Instead of using two pieces of natural wool to make a single color dump dye in three values, replace one piece with off-bolt colored wool or any other combination that you might like. It is another way to make similar yet different pieces of wool for your project.

The Citric Acid Step

If you add citric acid early in the process, whether by mixing it into the initial dye mixtures or by dissolving it in the host water, it will cause more pronounced mottling, because of all those peaks and valleys. If you add citric acid late in the process, at the end of step 5, the final product will have less mottling. The choice is a matter of taste and function. My version shown here was done with citric acid added early.

Dump Dyes

Version 2: Multicolor Dump Dye

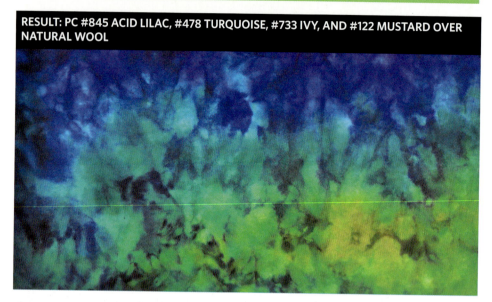

RESULT: PC #845 ACID LILAC, #478 TURQUOISE, #733 IVY, AND #122 MUSTARD OVER NATURAL WOOL

Dump dyes have an independent streak. Even when the utmost care is taken with the dye applications, colors break out and get a little rowdy. As that practice often ends up producing stunning wool, this is one of the few times you will ever find me affirming rowdy behavior. This piece of wool was made with 1/8 tsp. each of PC #845 Acid Lilac, PC #478 Turquoise, PC #733 Ivy, PC #122 Mustard in 2 cups water in four separate cups. Each cup of mixed dye was poured out in the order listed. Because the citric acid was added early, the mottling in this piece is quite pronounced.

If one color in three decreasing amounts of dye will make good wool, why not try the same process with three or four completely different colors?

Step 1: Cut 1 yard of wool and leave it in a single piece. Presoak the wool as you would for any method. When ready to dye, roughly fold/scrunch the wool from its long side, so that it evenly fits in a large steamer pan. Place the wool in the pan right side up if hooking the right side matters to you.

That amount is easy to reach when the spoon being used is 1/8 tsp. and the color number is four. When only three colors of dye are needed, I still use the 1/8 tsp., but I measure out three heaping 1/8 tsp. of dry dye. If you want much lighter wool, then drop down to the 1/16 tsp. measuring spoon.

Step 2: Select three or four dyes that go together well. Mix each color in its own mixing cup. The wool in the previous photo used four colors made from 1/8 tsp. of each dry dye listed (1/2 tsp. of total dye). According to our earlier discussions, 1/2 tsp. of dye will produce wool that is strong to medium in value. If you want wool that is this dark, combine measurements that come close to a total of 1/2 tsp. of dry dye.

Step 3: Using the same procedure as version 1, pour one color on each quadrant of the wool. The early addition of acid makes for more spots; late addition of the citric acid produces wool with less mottling. It is your choice.

Step 4: Cover the pan with a lid, and cook for 1 hour to set the wool.

This wool was made with three of the original colors used in the first example of version 2. PC #845 Acid Lilac, the darkest color of that first example, was left out of this pan. The rest of the original colors were used in $1/8$ tsp. amounts. Omitting one dye color produced significantly lighter wool. With more area to spread out—three color zones instead of four—each color could get out and mingle a little more, which resulted in less mottling. Less water, which would leave more peaks of wool sticking out of the surface, would have brought back more mottling because the dye would have had fewer places to go. Using $1/16$ tsp. of each dye would have produced even lighter wool.

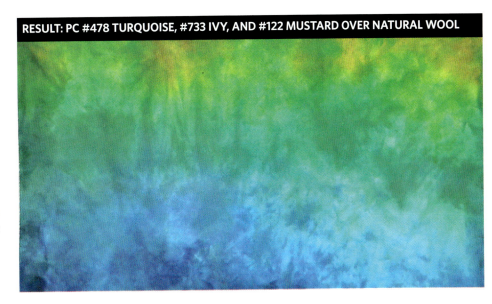

RESULT: PC #478 TURQUOISE, #733 IVY, AND #122 MUSTARD OVER NATURAL WOOL

This wool was made exactly like the others shown in version 2, based on $1/8$ tsp. of dye per color: PC #819 Purple, PC #808 Raspberry and PC #122 Mustard.

RESULT: PC #819 PURPLE, #808 RASPBERRY, AND #122 MUSTARD OVER NATURAL WOOL

Although PC #503 Brown, PC #719 Grasshopper, and PC #339 Lobster Bisque were used for this piece, any similar brown, yellow-green, and coral pink from another dye system would produce similar results. A change in pouring order (brown, green, lobster to brown, lobster, green) would also dramatically change the look of this trio and create a more natural progression than this example where the yellow green is in the middle. It is not that one way is right and the other is wrong. It is all about the look you want to create.

RESULT: PC #503 BROWN, #719 GRASSHOPPER, AND #339 LOBSTER BISQUE OVER NATURAL WOOL

Dump Dyes 103

RESULT: PC #811 BOYSENBERRY, #304 CAPE COD CRANBERRY, AND #235 PEACH OVER NATURAL WOOL

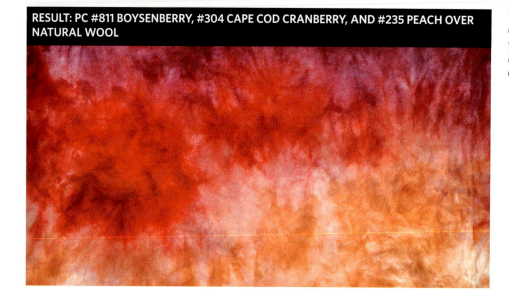

There is no end to the combinations that you can put together. This piece was made with ⅛ tsp. of PC #811 Boysenberry, PC #304 Cape Cod Cranberry, and PC #235 Peach Blossom.

The Monster Within

A 1-yard piece of wool can create such a pronounced balloon of wool that you might wonder what exactly is coming out of a cooking pan!

A bubble this high (I snapped it right as I took off the lid) renders the lid ineffective. It also removes the wool from contact with the dye solution. Once the lid is removed, the wool bubble will decrease, causing the wool to go back down into the water.

The bigger the piece of wool being dyed at one time, the bigger the hot air balloon that is created during the cooking process.

To tame the monster within, remember these rules:

- If there is color in the water, leave the lid off the pan to encourage the wool to stay in the bath until the wool takes in the color.
- Once the color has gone into the wool, the lid can be put back on the pan to help contain the heat and assist in the setting process.
- Since high heat makes for more steam and a bigger bubble, keep the burner turned as low as possible, but don't turn it so low that the water drops below the boiling point.
- If the wool keeps raising the lid, rotate the lid off center to make a crack for the steam to escape.
- Don't forget: with all that beautiful wool puffing out of the water, it might cover up a pan that is boiling dry. Where there is steam, you may be running out of water. Add water frequently to avoid scorching the wool.

Rowe Antique, 30" x 58", #8- and 8½-cut wool on burlap. Designed by House of Price; hooked by Robin Price, Angels Camp, California, 2012.
    The artist hooked the scrolls with wool from three different pieces of dump-dyed fabric that I created. While the three pieces did go together, they weren't necessarily made to go together. When two pieces share one color, a natural transition can usually be made if they are put together in the right sequence.

More variation from a single dump-dye session can be achieved if the wool comes from different bolts. In this case, I dyed several long ¼-yard pieces of different tweeds and plaids in one session. I'll admit these pieces look pretty wild. However, in the right spot, they look iridescent.

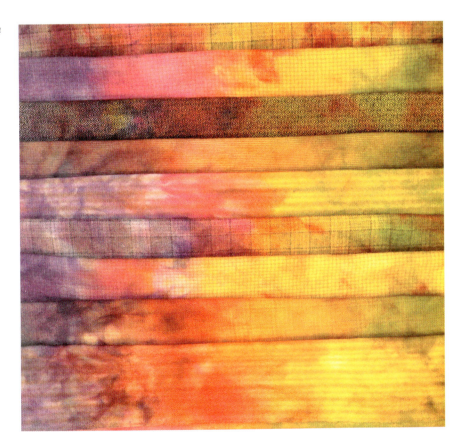

Dump Dyes 105

China Hen, 23" x 34 1/2", #4-, 5-, and 6-cut wool on monk's cloth. Designed by Gene Shepherd and hooked by Donna Bleam, Harrisonburg, Virginia, 2012.

The artist used some of the dump-dyed tweeds shown in the previous photo to hook the basket for this hen. Starting with the greenish end of a 1-yard-long strip, she began a little to the left of center, hooking her first horizontal strip from there to the right edge of the basket. This strip created a horizontal line with a color gradation of green to yellow to red to purple. A second 1-yard strip, which was tipped in a darker green, started out in the original "green hole" with the first piece but was hooked horizontally to the left, creating a similar, yet slightly darker, gradation. When she hooked adjacent strips in this repetitive fashion, the result was a lovely carnival glass basket with a great highlight.

Jumbo Star, 34" x 34", #7-cut wool and paisley on linen. Pattern by Lib Callaway; hooked by Janet Griffith, Frisco, Texas, 2011.

The center diamonds in the jumbo star were hooked from a dump-dye piece of wool made with just two colors—dark red and gold. The orange-red midsection was naturally created where those two colors mingled. Instead of cutting her wool with the selvedge, to create strips that bleed from red to orange to gold, Janet cut her wool against the grain. Not only did this give her longer strips (the width of the bolt), it also gave her three distinct sets of strips: dark red, orange, and gold. Thus, she was able to hook three rows of diamonds, each in a separate color. When working with a cut this size, it does not matter if the wool is cut with or against the selvedge. Photo by Janet Griffith

Trout Dreams (detail), #4- and 6-cut wool on cotton rug warp. Adapted, with permission, from a painting by Josh Udesen, Boise, Idaho, and hooked by Jean Coon, Corona Del Mar, California, 2012.

The striking coloration of each fish was achieved with dump-dyed wool cut against the selvedge.

Version 3: Dedicated Dumping

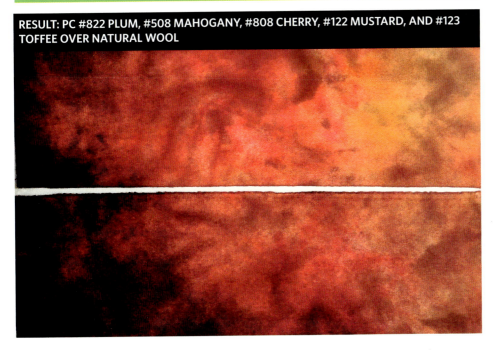

RESULT: PC #822 PLUM, #508 MAHOGANY, #808 CHERRY, #122 MUSTARD, AND #123 TOFFEE OVER NATURAL WOOL

If you dump in a very artistic, fruity way, the end result almost hooks itself. This method could just as easily be adapted, with other colors of course, to make wool for big pumpkins, peaches, or pears.

I use this method when making wool for students who want to hook a big piece of fruit, like the large pomegranates in one of my designs.

Step 1: This pan has two ¼-yard pieces cut using the long method. Each 36-inch piece is placed parallel to the other in the steamer pan. When placing the presoaked wool in the pan, make sure that the right side of the wool faces up so that it can accept the maximum amount of dye. Fill the pan with about 2 inches of water and 1 tsp. of citric acid granules. Bring the pan to a simmer.

Step 2: Five different colors of Pro Chem dye were used for this pan: #822 Plum, #508 Mahogany, #808 Cherry, #122 Mustard, and #123 Toffee. Mix each color with ⅛ tsp. to 2 cups boiling water in its own separate cup.

Dump Dyes 107

Step 3: Push the wool to the right to create some open space on the left side of the pan. Pour 2 cups of Mahogany in that open space. As the edge begins to make contact with the dye, use the tongs to nudge and reposition the wool so the entire edge makes good contact with the dye.

intermingle with the darker color while some of it proceeds to the right. Again, good tong work pays off. The goal is to gently move the dye along its graduated path but not in such a vigorous way as to completely cover the remaining wool.

I purposely moved more Raspberry toward the bottom of the pan than I did the top. I think it makes the wool look more "fruity." As that is the goal with this version—dedicated dumping to paint or create a large-sized version of a specific piece of fruit—pay close attention to where you pour the color. As you proceed, be gentle, but firm, creating valleys where necessary to stem the flow of dye! Even so, it is not unusual for the dye to travel on its own and end up in a surprise place or two. Since fruit has all sorts of blushing colors, a few surprises should add to the uniqueness of the wool.

the magic of the dye pan makes for much more interesting wool than we could ever contrive to make.

After about 20 to 30 seconds of cooking time, vigorously push the ends of the wool back to the left, into the original position against the left side of the pan. Pushing the wool to the left displaces the dye bath and sends it surging to the right. (You can practice this technique in your bathtub. If your body goes sliding to the back of a full tub, a wave of water will go surging in the opposite direction to the front.) While the dye bath moves to the right over the wool, the dye is being both sucked up by the waiting wool and diluted by the clear water it encounters. Both of those events will make a gradation of color values. Pay close attention to the wool as it may need a bit of help to ensure that the original color covers the first part of the pan.

Step 4: Add 2 cups of the second color, Raspberry. Pour it across the wool in an even manner at a "white" spot just to the right of where the first color ends. This pour will allow some of the Raspberry to bleed to the left and

Step 5: Now dump the third color, Mustard, in the upper right-hand corner of the pan. Let it sit undisturbed for about 30 seconds before nudging the wool over to the left to mingle with the Raspberry. Some of that dye can also be nudged down to the bottom right corner. Again, because dye has a mind of its own, some Raspberry traveled through the folds of the wool for secret rendezvous. That is all well and good as

Step 6: This photo shows the application of the last two colors of dye. Dump 2 cups Plum in the lower left-hand corner and allow the dye to set for about 30 seconds. Nudge some of that dye up the left side of the pan, but encourage most of it to proceed along the bottom right two-thirds of the pan. This creates a much darker side on that particular piece. The dark side can be used to hook the dark side of a pomegranate as it sits in a shadow. The lighter side (cooking on the top length of the pan) will be perfect for the side of the pomegranate that catches natural light.

The last color, Toffee, was applied in two spots. Most (half to a little more) of the dye went in the lower right corner, where it darkened the much brighter Mustard that was applied in step 5. Toffee was encouraged to mingle and spread out in much the same fashion as the other colors. However, the last bit of this dye was artistically spilt in three or four places on the red sections. If, like me, you spend time communing with pomegranates in the supermarket, you have certainly discovered that the fruit has highlights in every section. A little Toffee dumped here and there on the various red sections of the wool creates just such highlights.

Pomegrande (detail), #8-cut wool on linen. Designed by Gene Shepherd and hooked by Penny White, Agoura Hills, California, 2013.

A fruity dump dye created the vibrant wool for the pomegranates in this rug. The background is a mixture of the two lightest values of lazy swatch wool from PC #713 Olive Drab and pieces of marbleized wool from a twist of morning glory, sunflower, and mint and a second twist of morning glory, mint, and marigold.

Pomegrande Pillow, 17" square, #8-cut wool hooked on primitive linen. Designed by Gene Shepherd; hooked by Jean McEwen, Long Beach, California, 2012.

A dedicated dump dye created the highly specific wool used by the artist to hook the central motif. Even though the dye colors were applied to the wool in a regimented fashion, it is still up to the artist to pick and choose the specific strips he or she needs to make the fruit blush.

Version 4: Dump Dyes for Yarn

Dump dyes are an effective way to dye yarn if variegated coloration with a continual progressive repeat is what you want. That type of coloration works particularly well when producing yarn for a needle-punched leaf.

Step 1: Determine the lengths of yarn needed for punching a specific project, and then reconfigure a twist of natural yarn to that measurement. In this instance, my 2-by-4 pegged board, which takes 2 yards of length for one wrap, works very well. A length any longer would have trouble fitting in the steam pans. After wrapping the yarn, as described in part 1, soak the untwisted skein. When you are ready to dye, place the untwisted skein in a pan of simmering water. Add citric acid before any dye.

Step 2: Choose your colors, and mix them separately with boiling water. The amount of dye you use is dependent on both the amount of yarn being dyed and the desired value. This pan started with $1/8$ tsp. of PC #845 Acid Lilac poured over one end.

Step 3: The second dye color is $1/4$ tsp. PC #130 Caramel. Mix and then pour the dye in the middle of the yarn and allow the color to set 40 seconds before you encourage the dye to migrate to each end of the pan.

RESULT: PC #845 ACID LILAC AND #130 CARAMEL OVER NATURAL WOOL YARN

Caramel does double duty in this version by putting a wash over the purple end and a lighter finish on the opposite end.

Pickering Oak Leaf Pillow Top, *14" square, needle-punched bulky yarn on monk's cloth. Designed and punched by Gene Shepherd, Anaheim, California, 2012.*

All the leaf and acorn yarn for this punch project was made with dump-dyed wool. I had plenty of options because I dyed over long measured wraps of yarn, which allowed me to cut and punch precisely what was needed for any section.

Mini-Pickering Oak, *5" x 3", needle-punched wool thread on weaver's cloth. Designed by Gene Shepherd; punched by Iris Salter, Long Beach, California, 2012.*

The process needed to dye jumbo wool yarn is basically the same as that used for the fine wool thread used for this needle punch. Just adjust the amounts and utensils.

Because it takes such a small amount of fine wool thread to make a skein for needle punching, I recommend doing the entire dye process in aluminum foil. Measured sections of wool thread can be dump dyed right on the foil, then sealed and baked for 1 hour in a 250°F oven. Baking puts less stress on the delicate thread.

With a good dump dye, there is no limit to the number of color combinations you can make for fabric, yarn, or, in this case, fine thread.

DYEING WITH COMMERCIAL ACID DYE

batch 11

Dyeing for Animals

▼▼▼
The question: When dyeing for animals, which method should I use? Traditional multivalue swatch, lazy swatch, dip dye, spot dye, or dump dye? The answer: Yes: preferably all at once.
◂◂◂

Ways to Use Shaded Wool for Animals

- ▲ Accurate depiction of glossy coats and fur
- ▲ Capturing high contrast areas created by shadows
- ▲ Transition areas, like from the back to the tail

RESULT: PC #506 TAN OVER NATURAL WOOL

The variation in these tan and brown wools provides all the lights and darks needed to capture Molly's fur.

Animals, whether covered with hide, coat, or fur, shimmer and shine with a multiplicity of colors and values. To capture such subtleties, you do not need 6 to 12 values; you need 20 to 30! Even then, if you only use multiple values of one pure color, you will miss out on the surprise colors that often show up in shadows and highlights.

When my friend Elizabeth Black contacted me about dyeing wool for "some cows in my neighbor's pasture that I have wanted to hook for several years," she ended the request with, "You know what I want." As I have dyed quite a lot of wool for her and her students over the years, I did know exactly what she wanted:

- ▲ Multiple values of wool, light to dark, in the appropriate color family. In this case, it was Hereford Cow Red.
- ▲ Areas in each of those values with

Molly, 1995–2010, 15" x 15", #4- and 5-cut wool on linen. Designed and hooked by Sarah Province, Silver Spring, Maryland, 2012. (Wool dyed by Gene Shepherd.)

Sarah hooked this piece as a memorial rug for Molly's owner, Judie Pasquin. Although different colors and strengths of dye were used, the dog wool in Molly was created with the same process (but a different dye recipe) as that used for the Hereford cow wool in this section's demonstration.
Photo by Laura Pierce

spots, dribbles, and other markings suitable to the animal being hooked. Wool marked in this way will create, when cut, subdivisions of values within general sections of color.
- Spots of colorful, yet appropriate, highlights in other color families. When studying a visual, if a dark shadow has a black, green, or purplish look to it, add some spots of that unexpected color to at least one section of the wool being dyed.
- A generous amount of wool so that there are plenty of options from which to pick.

Consequently, to make wool suitable for hooking purebred Hereford cows, I used a hybrid method of dyeing that combines the elements of a lazy swatch, dump dye, and spot dye.

Dyeing for Animals 113

Step 1: Use ½-yard pieces of wool cut on the selvedge at 18 inches then torn the entire width of the bolt. I needed two pieces of that size for one batch in the steamer pan. Although natural wool was fine for the tones of the Hereford cows, some colors that could be affected by the tawny nature of natural will end up better if white wool is used. All wool should be presoaked in water with a little Synthrapol.

Step 2: Select whichever colors you need for your particular project. My base color for the cows was PC #130 Caramel—1½ tsp. of dye mixed in 2 cups boiling water. As I could see a purplish cast to some of the dark shadows in the cows, as well as some golden highlights in lighter sections, I also mixed up ¼ tsp. of PC #822 Plum to 1 cup water and ¼ tsp. of PC #122 Mustard to 2 cups water.

Step 3: Place one ½-yard piece of wool, top side up and scrunched to fit, in a steamer casserole pan with 2 inches of water. Add a bit of citric acid to the pan, and turn on the heat.

Step 4: Starting at the right-hand side of the pan, apply your base dye mixture. Carefully pour from top to bottom (on the short side) in zebra-like stripes or lines, to about the midpoint of the pan. Use about ½ cup of the dye solution. Don't be so energetic in your pouring as to cause the dye to run all over the pan. Try to keep it semicontained on the right side. After 1 to 2 minutes of cooking, push all the peaks of wool under the water and pour another ½ cup over the same area as before. Let this second application also cook for 2 minutes.

Step 5: Use a pair of tongs to reposition the dyed section of wool to expose any undyed areas in that section. Once exposed, push them under the bath so that they can soak up the dye. Do a quick spot application of dye to those sections.

Step 6: Add 1 cup water to the remaining dye solution and then start striping the left side of the pan in the same method as before. It will take a few minutes to do this.

Step 7: When all the dye has been added to the pan, gently double check the wool for white spots. Push those areas below the water. Even after a few minutes of cooking, don't be surprised if there is still some dye in the pan.

Step 8: If you want highlights on the wool, add them now. I spotted a little Plum along the far right edge of the pan. I spotted some of the Mustard on the lighter left side of the pan. Once the spotting is done, leave the wool undisturbed for a few minutes to allow the concentration of that color to go into the fabric. If the initial spots seem too strong, use tongs to wiggle the wool enough to dissipate the color.

At this stage in the process, a bolt-wide piece of wool has been dyed to have a gradation that runs from very dark to dark, with a few sections of Plum and Mustard highlights.

It will take more than just a few values of rust-colored wool to recreate this beautiful Hereford cow from Bunting Farm in Albion, Illinois.

TIP	MORE OPTIONS ARE ALWAYS BETTER

You can never have too many options of colored wool when hooking an animal. One way to increase those options is to use slightly different colors of base wool. The same dye bath described here, if used with a combination of lights—white, natural, beige, and pale yellow—will produce an even broader selection of options. This is particularly good for home dyers who want to use up smaller pieces of odd wool from their stashes. When arranging such pieces in the pan before dyeing, remember to place the darker pieces in the areas that will receive the darker concentrations of dye.

Step 9: Using tongs, push the first piece of wool to the right side of the pan, creating enough space to add the new, second piece of wool. This much wool in this small space will require a lot of scrunching. Unattached dye in the water of the pan will quickly be absorbed into the folds of the new wool, usually producing fabric with some nice streaks of color. Add a couple more inches of water to the pan.

Step 10: If you want deeper colors of wool, as was my case for the Hereford cows, mix up another 1/2 tsp. of the base color (PC #130) in 2 cups water. At the spot where the two pieces of wool meet, pour about half of the newly mixed dye. Use the tongs to help the new dye move in each direction. Add more dye to the lighter sections, as needed, until they look right to your eye. While you won't need to add Plum to the light sections, some selective spot dyeing with a weakened mixed dye (Mustard or another gold) will bring some highlights to the piece. Any amount of tweaking can be done at any time by adding base or highlight dyes. Once the wool is right to your eye, cover the pot and cook the wool for 1 hour.

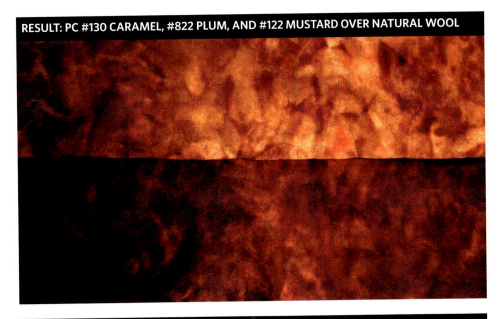

The two 18-inch bolt-wide pieces are shown together to show the full dark to light progression. To use this wool, the artist will tear it into several sections: darkest, really dark, dark, kinda dark, medium, etc.

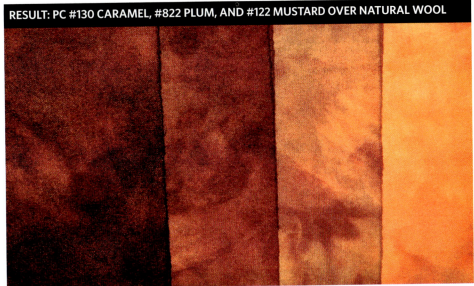

Once the value sections are torn in six 10-inch pieces, they can be arranged in their sequential value order. Just four of the Hereford wool strips are shown here in value sequence, light to dark. Once arranged, these wide sections can then be cut and kept together in groups until you are ready to use them. Think of them as a really big, oddly mottled swatch. Even so, when hooking any section of an animal, you will need to carefully look at your strips for just the right piece.

Dyeing for Animals

The Ladies Are at the Beach, *34" x 60", #3- and 4-cut wool on cotton rug warp. Designed and hooked by Elizabeth Black, Bentonville, Virginia, 2012. (The Hereford wool in this rug was dyed by Gene Shepherd.)*

    In assessing the wool provided for this project, Elizabeth said: "This wool gave me all the variations I needed. As I never know exactly what I will want for a project until I get into it, it was wonderful to have so many options of both color and value. At any time during the creative process, when something special was needed to make a certain area pop, all I had to do was start picking through all those options for just that right piece. While some people might have avoided this wool because it seemed to have too many contrasts, I think that the artist can't ever have too many options. It is the options that make it possible for us to bring not only contrast, but real depth, to our work."

Maggie Sue, 14½" x 16½", #3- and 4-cut wool on unbleached linen. Designed and hooked by Carla Jensen, Clovis, California, 2012.

The wool for Maggie Sue *came from the same recipe that was used for* Molly. However, more of the darker pieces of wool were needed for the basset hound than for the cocker spaniel.

I used ½ tsp. of PC #506 Tan to 2 cups water over two ½-yard pieces of wool to make the wool for Molly. Although the process was basically the same as that previously described, an extensive peak and valley system provided the odd surprise colors without any additional colors being added as spots. When peaks are kept out of the dye bath for the first 1 to 2 minutes into the cooking time, it effectively rearranges colors in the same way as with the delayed entry of lazy swatch pieces. This happens, as described in batch 4, because the various colors of the dye bath go into the wool in a staggered order: blue, red, and then yellow. When a peak, which sticks above the bath, goes in a little late, it misses the early-entry colors. When it eventually does take the plunge, there will be fewer colors in lesser amounts for it to accept.

RESULT: PC #506 TAN OVER NATURAL WOOL

Dyeing for Animals 117

DYEING WITH COMMERCIAL ACID DYE

batch 12

Stacked Pot

RESULT: PC #845 ACID LILAC, #338 MAGENTA, #407 SKY BLUE, AND #122 MUSTARD OVER ASSORTED WOOL

The wool in this stacked pot was made with PC #845 Acid Lilac, #338 Magenta, #407 Sky Blue, and #122 Mustard over approximately 2 to 3 yards of miscellaneous wool pieces.

▲▲▲

Who says you have to be in charge of every pot? If you give the dye and wool room for creative expression, you'll end up with a wonderful stash of beautiful colors.

▼▼▼

Ways to Use Stacked Pot Wool

- Great way to repurpose found wool
- Like a spot dye, without the time and effort
- Wonderful fruit
- Wonderful leaves
- Wonderful vegetation
- Anytime wool with surprise colors is needed

While the term "stacked pot" is an apt description of this method, "surprise pot" would be just as appropriate. If you think any of the previous dye batches described in this book were a little too spontaneous, you ain't seen nothing yet!

I like to make a stacked pot on the days when I just need to have a little fun in the dye kitchen. We are usually overly focused on rigid steps and measurements that will achieve certain prescribed ends. It is liberating to produce a large pot of wool that surprises with a multiplicity of colors and values. True, it is possible to tip a stacked pot in a specific direction. In fact, I often do that. However, the genius of a stacked pot rests in our ability to relax and let the pot and dye do their work.

Step 1: Assemble 2½ to 3 yards of wool fabric in a mixture of solids, colored, and textured fabric. Soak the colors and textures separately.

Right: Twisted Stripes, *14" x 6", hooked and braided #8-cut wool on linen. Designed and made by Susan L. Feller, Augusta, West Virginia, 2012.*

This piece was inspired by the cotton fabric used as backing and for mounting the piece on stretcher bars. The artist chose to use more braiding than hooking in this piece because that technique showed more of the wool's surface and thus did a better job enhancing the look of the wool.

Step 2: Select four colors of dye. This version will use PC #845 Acid Lilac, PC # 338 Magenta, PC #407 Sky Blue, and PC #122 Mustard. Mix ¼ tsp. dye of each color with 1 cup boiling water in separate measuring cups and set aside.

Step 6: Immediately add another handful of soaked pieces to the pot. No extra water needs to be added. Use the tongs to poke the second layer of wool into the existing dye bath. The peaks will be half in, half out.

With any repositioning, always make sure to quickly poke all surface wool under the bath so it has time to interact with that section of the dye.

Step 3: Pour the darkest color (Acid Lilac) into a saucepan. Fill it with boiling water and add ½ tsp. of citric acid. Follow this step before adding each dye color to the pot.

Step 4: Put about ½ yard of soaked fabric pieces in a large dye pot. (I just grab a big handful as they come out of the soaking bath.) Add enough water, about 2 inches, so that the wool is not quite covered. Bring the water to a boil.

Step 5: When the water is boiling, quickly dump in the saucepan of mixed dark dye. Use tongs to gently prod the wool so the dye mixture can come in contact with all the wool. Although you do not want white spots, you also do not want to vigorously stir the wool.

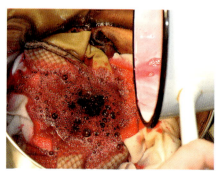

Step 7: Prepare a saucepan full of the second color (#338 Magenta) following the directions in step 3 and quickly dump it into the dye pot. Once again, use the tongs to slightly reposition the wool so the new dye not only makes general contact with the new pieces but also has the opportunity to trickle down into the first layer. I help this interaction by inserting the tongs through the layers of wool to a lower section of the stack, pinching some wool at that level and moving it up and down a couple of inches. Should you feel there is not enough interaction of color between layers, pull up a few peaks from the bottom layer into the new color mix.

Step 8: Immediately add a third group of pieces and punch them into the previous mixture as described. The last color of dye should be noticeable as it starts to affect the new wool.

Step 9: Quickly dump the saucepan of Mustard over this third layer and repeat all the instructions for helping the new layer make contact with the dye while encouraging some limited migration of color throughout the other layers of the pot.

At any time, particularly when the goal is to make wool for a certain project, it is fine to be more aggressive. If the red layer is looking too red for a leaf you wish to hook, bring up bigger sections of the red into the Mustard bath so that the red can go orange. Always make adjustments quickly, and always end by pushing the wool under the dye bath.

Step 11: Keep adding layers of wool and color in this fashion until the pot is either full or you have run out of prepared wool.

Whatever final color you choose, this last application requires a better, overall stir to reposition everything for the final hour of cook time.

Often, I end the layering with a final bath of a color I think would unify each layer of the stack. Often, it is a yellow—in this case, Mustard.

Step 10: Add more wool and the fourth color (Sky Blue) in the same way that previous colors were added.

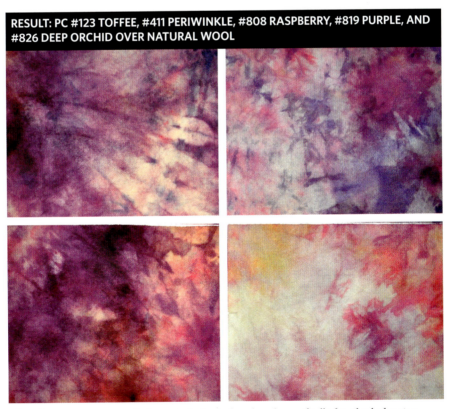

These four pieces came out of a large stacked pot of wool made specifically for a hooked project featuring grapes. While purples, blues, reds, and yellows were still used for the various layers, the specific dyes chosen for each layer were different than our original example. Additionally, a little more rearrangement, layer to layer, took place before each new dye was added. If you are dyeing with a specific project in mind, it is easy to tip a pot in whatever direction you want the color to go.

RESULT: PC #845 ACID LILAC, #338 MAGENTA, #407 SKY BLUE, AND #122 MUSTARD OVER ASSORTED WOOLS

RESULT: PC #121 MAPLE SUGAR, #495 TEAL, #713 OLIVE DRAB, #709 HERB GREEN, AND #822 PLUM OVER MIXED PIECES

With historic vegetation as the goal, softer colors of plum, various greens, a little blue, and a couple of golds were used to make the stacked pots that produced this sampling of pieces.

A stacked pot is particularly effective when you need to repurpose found wool. This odd assortment of wool, many pieces from garments older than I am, is just the sort of thing many fiber artists seem to attract by the garbage bag full. We can't throw the wool away, but there isn't enough of any one to inspire a project. When preparing wool for a historical re-creation for the Frost Collection of the Hooked Rug Museum of North America, using odds and ends seemed appropriate for the remaking of an 1880s hooked rug that required a lot of leaves and stems. Fiber artists from New England would have used such wool in their rugs. To that end, garbage bags of old wool were opened and repurposed with a stacked pot.

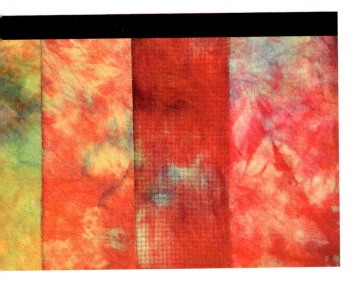

This progression of wool shows a selection of pieces that came out of each layer of this stacked pot session. Because they are arranged in layer order (purple, red, yellow, blue, yellow) the interplay of colors between each stack is obvious. Had only natural wool been used for this stack, there would have been a more pronounced and regular color progression. Still, I like the surprise colors that I get when an odd piece of Marigold wool ends up in the darkest purple bath.

Welcome (detail), 34" x 28", #4-, 5-, 6-, and 8-cut wool on Scottish burlap. Designed by Edward Sands Frost; hooked by Teresa Heinze, Lubbock, Texas, 2012, for the Hooked Rug Museum of North America.

This piece was hooked with overdyed vintage wool. When asked about the suitability of the stacked pot wool for the leaves in this project, the artist replied: "It really proves that you can make a silk purse out of a sow's ear!" Photo by Naomi Hill

There's only one problem I've found with stacked pot wool. Before this particular stacked pot, I had a garbage bag of wool that I was ready to toss because I needed the space. Now, after the pot, I have a garbage bag of wool I like that I have to find a place to store!

Stacked Pot 123

DYEING WITH COMMERCIAL ACID DYE

batch 13

Ordered Casserole Pancake

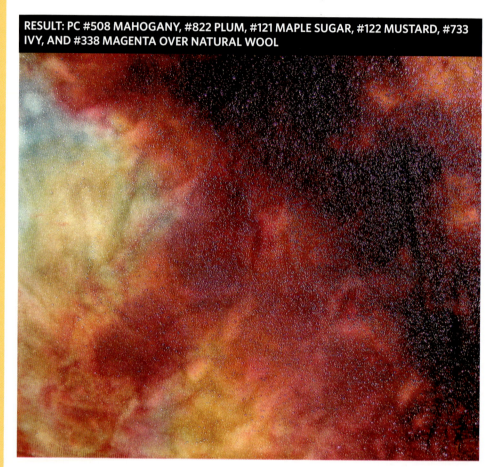

RESULT: PC #508 MAHOGANY, #822 PLUM, #121 MAPLE SUGAR, #122 MUSTARD, #733 IVY, AND #338 MAGENTA OVER NATURAL WOOL

▲▲▲ Hook this wool in the order it was cut to render subtle color transitions. ▲▲▲

This bottom layer of "pancake" wool was artistically spotted with tablespoons of individually mixed dyes—PC #508 Mahogany, #822 Plum, #121 Maple Sugar, #122 Mustard, #733 Ivy, and #338 Magenta ($1/16$ tsp. to 1 cup of boiling water each). A beautiful piece of wool like this just begs to be used to hook a fall leaf. If not hooked sequentially, however, the blocks of colors in the wool will not end up next to each other. Instead of creating a leaf with natural sections of color bleeding into each other, a randomly hooked leaf would take on a stripy appearance.

Ways to Use Ordered Casserole Pancake Wool

- Leaves
- Fruit
- Stained glass
- Hooked and prodded flowers
- A good way to make several similar pieces

Any wool cooked in a casserole pan is, technically, a casserole dye. However, I prefer names that are more descriptive. In this case, individual layers of wool are spot dyed in a casserole pan, like a stack of pancakes, then cooked together until set. While the beautiful wool produced can be hooked hit and miss, its particular genius becomes apparent when the strips are hooked in the order they were cut. Thus, this section is about the "ordered casserole pancake" method.

Pickering Oak Leaf Pillow, *18" square, #6- and 8-cut wool on monk's cloth. Designed and hooked by Gene Shepherd, Anaheim, California, 2006.*

A separate piece of ordered casserole pancake wool was used to hook each of the leaves in this design. By hooking the strips in the order they were cut, all the color sections of the wool were kept together.

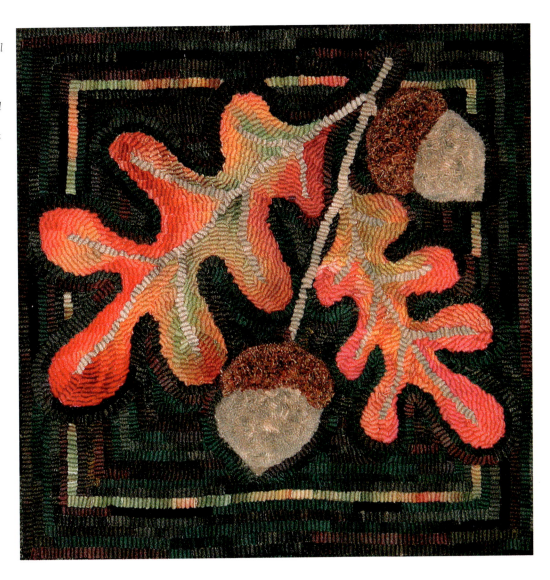

Version 1: Making Leaves

Step 1: Measure the length and width of the pan's bottom, and prepare pieces of wool fabric that will fit within those dimensions.

While pieces of wool can be smaller than either dimension of the pan, they should not be bigger. Each piece needs to lie flat with no edges riding up on the sides of the pan. This white enamel antique icebox drip pan can handle an entire $1/8$-yard piece of wool. Most other pans, however, need pieces that have been trimmed especially for them. Odd-sized remnants of wool are perfect for this process. If smaller pieces of wool will work for your project, try an electric skillet instead of a casserole pan. Once the pieces are torn to fit the size of the pan, presoak them in hot water with some softening agent.

Step 2: Choose your dye colors based on your project. When doing smaller pieces of wool (8" x 8" or 8" x 10"), five colors of dye are probably enough for an interesting leaf. If the wool pieces are larger (14½" x 18", as shown), then additional colors can be used. While I pick those colors on a whim, I usually have at least one each of hot yellow, dull gold, brighter red, plum, teal, blue, and green. If you are planning 6 to 10 layers of wool, mix up each color in a separate cup, ⅛ tsp. to 2 cups boiling water. Add a little citric acid to each cup.

Step 3: Place one piece of wool in the bottom of the pan. If you are dyeing a small piece of wool with just five colors, you can do something as simple as spoon or pour a separate color in each corner, with the fifth color going in the center. As the colors mingle, new variations will form on their own. I usually start in one corner with a light color and go from there.

It is difficult for me to not play with all my colors, creating individual pieces of wool that I think will make good leaves. Most of the time, I apply my colors in a dark to light theme. This particular pan suggests gold for the edge of a leaf, progressing into darker blue greens. Sometimes I pour and other times I spoon a little here and a little there until things look right to my eye. Do remember, however, that multiple colors applied in this fashion will mingle and calm down a bit during the cooking process.

Having Trouble Selecting Dye Colors for Leaves?

If you just can't figure out what colors would make a good leaf, go on a walk and gather some leaf visuals! In the leaf on the left, I see PC Mustard, Golden Yellow, Bright Red, MochaChino, Mahogany, Avocado, and Plum. If using Cushing Dye for the leaves on the right, I would use Turkey Red, Crimson, Orange, Buttercup Yellow, and Plum.

Not only do leaves suggest color choices, they also suggest the patterns by which those choices can be poured or spooned on the wool. Nature is usually bolder in both color and pattern than most of us would dare to be.

Bottom line for leaf colors: If you can imagine the colors together, you can probably find a leaf with those colors.

Step 4: Once a layer has been colored, place a new piece of fabric directly on top of the last one. Don't be surprised if some of the previously applied dye starts to bleed through the fabric; color will run both horizontally and vertically through the various pieces of wool. Although it is a good idea to re-spot with colors and values in the basic areas where they were placed on the previous piece (yellows over yellows, blues over blues, lights over lights and darks over darks, etc.), this process is very relaxed. New colors can be added at any level and old ones removed.

Step 5: After making five or six layers with the original dye mixtures, the measuring cups of dye should be about half full. If you continue using these dyes as is, all the leaf pieces will be similar to those already colored. If you need greater variation, top off all the cups of dye with enough clear water to bring the level back up to the 2-cup mark.

Adding more water to the mix will lighten each color, thereby creating leaf pieces in a lighter value than those on the bottom of the stack. While I added water halfway through the process in this example, a more gradual gradation of dark to lighter pieces can be achieved by topping off the cup of dye every two or three layers. In this particular example, I did not like the abruptness of the change because not all of the colors toned down enough.

Step 6: At any time, should you feel the spots are a little too abrupt, as was the case with the last step shown, a little extra splash of yellow or boiling water will smooth out the rough color edges. That adjustment corrected this piece by blending the colors better than the initial pour did.

Another good source of blending dye is the growing pool of excess dye on the edges of the pan. In those surface areas of the fabric where a little extra dye is needed, use a spoon to baste the wool with these "dye drippings."

Step 7: When all the layers have been colored, you'll need to make a decision about the excess dye in the pan. If left as is, all four sides of the wool will soak up the excess dye, creating a very dark edge. Since several colors of dye have gone into the pan, the edge wool usually ends up in a very dark brownish red color. If you like that look, leave the excess dye alone. On occasion, I use such edges for veins in the leaves hooked with this wool.

I usually want as much leaf wool as possible, so I normally remove the excess dye. By holding all the wool at one corner with my thumb, I can tip the pan so that all the excess dye can be poured out without disturbing the layers of the wool. It can either go down the drain or be saved for a batch of reddish brown wool. Once the excess dye is gone, pour in a cup of clear vinegar and enough water to keep the wool moist during the hour-long cooking process.

Cover the casserole pan with a lid or aluminum foil, and bake the batch in a 300°F oven for 1 hour. At the end of the cooking process, all liquid left in the pan should be clear.

Just like leaves on a tree, the wool will be similar yet different.

Version 2: Separating Layers with Different Colors

You may want to make related yet decidedly different pieces of wool for a project. Some layers may be so bold that they will, unless stopped, affect other layers. So you'll want to bring in an obstacle to keep the colors separate.

Step 1: Using the dominant petal from my visual aid (below) as my inspiration, I started on the bottom (darkest) piece with a bold splash of PC #808 Raspberry. The darker spots on that blush were colored with a slight application of salt dye (see the sidebar for an explanation). PC #121 Maple Sugar and PC #122 Mustard were also used to complete the coloration of this piece.

Step 2: To preserve all that detail from the first layer, make a color barrier by carefully covering the entire dyed layer with four pieces of interfolded deli wrap. While these 10-by-10 3/4-inch pieces of paper usually come to us wrapped around a sandwich, they are readily available without the sandwich in grocery and restaurant stores. They are touted as being "microwave safe, grease resistant with wet strength added," but the manufacturer would probably be glad to know that they are perfect for stopping color from moving among layers of dyed wool.

Once a layer has been covered with the paper, place the next piece of wool in the stack. Paper only needs to go between layers that are decidedly different or delicate.

Successive layers can also be easily lightened just by adding a little clear water to the dye mixture before each new layer is colored.

My visual for this batch of wool was a rose in my wife's garden. I wanted to do one batch of wool that would produce ordered pieces that would replicate the strong central blush of hot pink on the dominant petal, some medium blush wool for the side petals, and other pieces much lighter, yet with little to no blush. As I did not want to spend a lot of time and wool making several pieces, I got everything done with just four pieces, or layers of wool, in one pan.

Salt Dye

Salt dye can be made by combining any dry powdered dye with coarse Kosher salt. For an easy application, I keep some cheap, dollar store saltshakers on hand. When I need some delicate flecks in a piece of dyed wool, I fill an empty shaker half full of salt and $\frac{1}{64}$ tsp. of whichever dye I want to use. Then I stir the mix with the handle of a spoon so the dye powder gets evenly distributed over the salt crystals. If "salted" over a piece of wet wool, the crystals will deliver a burst of color wherever they land.

As the appearance of color is a delayed reaction, go light when adding salt dye to a piece of wool. Once applied, if the fabric is moved, that too will move the intense burst of color, causing runs or streaks on the wool. Consequently, unless you want that sort of movement, don't disturb a salted piece of wool.

Many leaves have tiny speckles of color all over them, and a salt dye is a great way to replicate that look. When a project is done, I label the saltshaker with the dye color name and place it in an airtight container until I need it again.

Of course, salt dyes are not just for speckles and streaks. Shakers at the ready in a variety of colors can quickly add a little bit of seasoning to any pot or pan of dye that just needs . . . something. It is particularly helpful when all the mixed dye has already gone into the pot but you still want more color. A shake here and there—with this and that—can color white spaces that don't have enough dye or add highlights and blushes to suit your every need.

RESULT: PC #808 RASPBERRY, #121 MAPLE SUGAR, AND PC #122 MUSTARD OVER NATURAL WOOL

By separating each of the four layers in this one batch, four very unique pieces of wool were produced in one operation. Without the paper barrier, both color and detail would have blended too much in the cooking process.

To reproduce the look of this particular rose, the first (and darkest) piece would have to be hooked in ordered fashion to keep all the detailed coloration of the wool in place. While secondary blushes would also have to be hooked in that same way, the rest of the partial petals showing could be hooked with the appropriate golden sections of the wool.

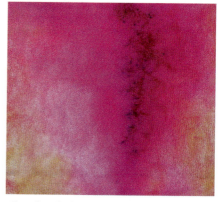

This detailed shot of the first layer shows what it looks like after being dyed and dried. I made the deep speckled shadow with the salt dye. Again, all this detail will be lost unless the cut strips are hooked in their sequential order. Since replicating the center dark slash of color is the primary goal, I would tear this piece down the middle to begin. From that middle tear, I would cut strips and sequentially hook them from the center out to each side. This will preserve the central blush and is a better plan for this particular project than starting on one side and working to the other.

Version 3: Repetitive Similar Pieces

Step 2: After the first piece is dyed, add a second layer on top and dye the wool as before.

On those occasions when you need multiple—but not necessarily identical—pieces of similar wool, the ordered pancake method is an easy way to stack up a good supply.

Step 1: Lay the first piece of wool in the pan, then strategically spoon sections of yellow, red, and finally blue dyes onto the wool, leaving some white space between the colors. I usually eyeball the placement of color for something like this, but if you wish to be precise, measure the wool piece beforehand to make sure you get the color in the right spot. To connect the colors, add enough additional dye at each color junction to encourage mingling.

The second piece is much easier because color placement has already been worked out in the previous piece. Dye from the first layer will probably even bleed up enough to show the places where each color goes. Even so, this does not have to be an exact, precise placement. It just needs to be close.

Make as many layers as needed—or as many as the casserole pan will hold—in one batch. All the layers will end up being a little different but similar.

I made this batch for a repetitive rainbow background, but it could be used for any multicolored progression. Once again, this progression would have been lost were it not for the fact that the wool was cut on the short side of the piece and then hooked in order.

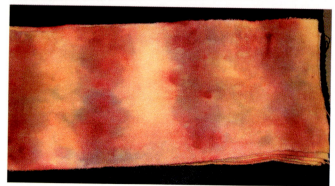

Black-eyed Susan wool, a simple repetitive ordered pancake process, does not look too great before it is shaped and prodded! Still, because the end product would be cut and shaped, it was a pretty easy job to mark and spot the wool so the reddish color would be at the throat of the petals and the gold would be at the tip. The first layer is the hardest. After that, it is just as easy to make 10 pieces as it is two.

Prairie Blooms *(detail), prodded by Mary Lynne Gehrett, 2011 (see the full rug on page 68). The prodded flowers were made with shaped ordered pancake wool on linen backing. The black-eyed Susan blossoms definitely benefited from a good pancake dye.*

Pomegrande, 24" x 16½", wool appliqué with embroidery embellishments. Designed by Gene Shepherd; made by Barbara Holden, Long Beach, California, 2012.

The artist used pancake wool for the pomegranates and border. Marbleized wool was used for the host background of this piece. The frame and leaves came from different values of a lazy swatch.

Need to make wool that looks like stained glass? Use the ordered pancake method.

Few things are more fun to dye than pieces of wool that look like stained glass. It is very easy to dye three or four layers with one set of colors, then add a new color to the mix for three or four more, adding and changing out colors until an entire pan is dyed. Strong color variation between layers means you'll need a barrier of deli wrap to contain a roving color.

Wm. Pickering Oak Appliqué Mat, *12" x 18", appliquéd wool with embroidered embellishments. Designed by Gene Shepherd; made by Jan Winter, Hollywood, California, 2012.*

Ordered pancake is equally good for appliqué projects—particularly those that require multiple pieces of similar wool.

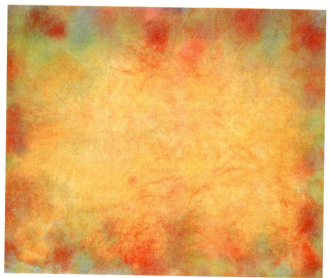

This large piece of wool, carefully dyed to be the border on the Pickering Oak project, started life as the bottom layer of a pancake batch of wool.

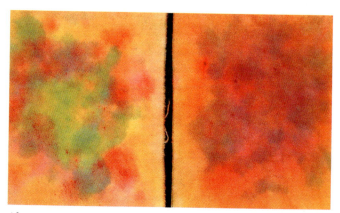

After covering the bottom layer with deli wrap, several smaller pieces of wool were dyed and stacked to make the fabric for the fall leaves.

DYEING WITH COMMERCIAL ACID DYE

Dyeing Mohair

batch 14

RESULT: MAGENTA, SKY BLUE, MUSTARD, AND PURPLE OVER NATURAL MOHAIR

Spoonfuls of Magenta, Sky Blue, Mustard, and Purple spread out and mingle to create a beautiful rainbow of colors.

▲▲▲
Hand-dyed mohair makes a luminous addition to any project fortunate enough to get it.
▼▼▼

If wool fleece can be dyed once it's woven or spun into fabric or yarn, then it stands to reason that it can also be dyed straight from the sheep. This is particularly good when the sheep in question is a mohair sheep with luscious curly locks.

Such extravagant fiber adds excitement to any art piece. While the general process for dyeing mohair—or any other fleece—is the same as dyeing wool fabric and yarn, there are some special considerations.

Ways to Use Dyed Fleece

◢ Embellishment of hooked projects
◢ Needle felting
◢ Knitting, crocheting, and spinning

Cleaning the Fleece before Dyeing

Believe it or not, this is considered clean fleece. I pay more to get it this clean, which makes me wonder what it would look like if it were not clean!

Dyeing Mohair 135

Homage to Joseph, 10" x 12", #6- and 8-cut wool with mohair embellishments and #12-cut knotted details on primitive linen. An adaptation of J is for Joseph, originally designed and hooked by Patty Yoder. Made by Gene Shepherd, 2012, with permission from the Patty Yoder family.

I remember well the first copy of Rug Hooking magazine I ever saw because it contained a photo of Patty Yoder's wonderful rainbow sheep Joseph. As my eyes locked on those vibrant colors, my jaw hit the ground! I have felt empowered to use color ever since. When I needed an illustration for a way to use mohair, this was the perfect way to say thank you to Patty for her inspiration.

When Dyeing Mohair . . .

- A little mixed dye goes a long way. If you are using several colors in one dye pan, you'll need only very small amounts of each color in ½ cup boiling water.

- Mohair is very efficient in gobbling up dye color; don't underestimate it.

- If initial spots of color seem to be too dark, add a little more water to the dye mixture before continuing.

- When spotting, it is better to start out underdoing as opposed to overdoing. More dye can always be added to your pan, but give the colors a chance to mingle on their own before making those additions. My least favorite pans of dyed mohair are the ones where I put in too much color. That said, do remember that mohair, like all other fiber, will look darker when it is wet than after it has cooked and dried.

Step 1: As clean fleece is not clean enough to start dyeing, the mohair has to be gone over a handful at a time to pick out all bits of straw, dirt, sheep manure, and weed residue. Until I started dyeing mohair, I never really understood the ramifications of the sedate reference in my great great grandmother's Club Diaries from 1923: *Had all the ladies from the church over to spend the afternoon picking wool.* If you have a lot of mohair to dye, I would suggest you make a casserole and invite a group of friends over for this fun, old-fashioned event. Don't tell them everything they are picking out unless they ask—and make sure they wash their hands before they eat!

As another way of illustrating the care with which one should pick over the mohair, four or five handfuls of wool were picked over a cloth so that the amount of loose residue would show up. As jobs go, I can certainly think of worse. It just takes a little effort to carefully sort each clump of wool without disturbing the delicate curls. If you don't get it out before you dye, the debris won't go away. It will still show up after the dye session is finished. The wool naturally comes in clumps or clusters of fiber, so don't overpick whilecleaning. Do your best to preserve the natural integrity of those beautiful curls.

Step 2: Once the wool is properly picked over, transfer it to a shallow pan of warm water with Synthrapol. Make sure the water level is deep enough to completely submerge the mohair. Let the fleece soak for 1 to 2 hours in a sudsy bath. Every so often, use your hand to push the fleece under the water. Gentle agitation in this fashion, during a long soak, will release unwanted particles you may have missed during the first inspection. Don't be surprised if you find a lot of residue at the bottom of this pan.

Step 3: Transfer the mohair into a large colander, one handful at a time, squeezing it to remove the dirty water. Yes, it would be easier to pour the pan of soaked wool into the colander, but doing so would just redistribute the residue from the soak. Once in the colander, rinse the wool with clear water. The easiest way is to immerse the colander/mohair in a sink of clear water. The colander will contain the wool, allowing any residual dirt to be swept away.

After the final rinse, place a single layer of mohair in a shallow casserole pan. Add warm water so the liquid level comes to the top of the fiber. Place the pan on a heat source and bring the water to a simmer.

Step 4: As the mohair cooks on the stove, begin spotting with your choice of mixed dye colors. I used $1/64$ tsp. each of PC #338 Magenta, PC #490 Brilliant Blue, PC #407 Sky Blue, PC #122 Mustard, PC #119 Sun Yellow, and PC #819 Purple to $1/2$ cup boiling water each.

Step 5: After spotting the mohair to your satisfaction, add more boiling water to the pan to ensure that it can't boil dry during the cook time. Also add some citric acid or clear vinegar. Cover the batch with a lid, and place the pan in a preheated 300°F oven for 1 hour.

Step 6: Transfer the mohair to the colander and rinse it twice, plunging the whole thing up and down in the water. Keep the mohair in the colander the whole time. It can easily get away from you if you don't take that safeguard. Let the mohair drain by removing the colander from the rinse and setting it aside.

Step 7: Remove the mohair from the colander, one natural cluster at a time. Squeeze each cluster in your fist; then taking hold of the cut side, give the cluster a good shake or two. Much like the way a dog fluffs his wet coat with a couple of shakes, this will fluff the mohair and encourage those curls to reform.

Step 8: Place the shaken curls in a sheltered place where they can air dry.

Know Your Mohair

Each cluster of mohair has two sides:

- ▲ The cut side. This part was closest to the sheep before it was sheared. It tends to be a little more matted and flattened.

- ▲ The curly side. These lovely, perfect locks were furthest from the body of the sheep.

RESULT: PC #338 MAGENTA, #490 BRILLIANT BLUE, #407 SKY BLUE, #122 MUSTARD, #119 SUN YELLOW, AND #819 PURPLE OVER NATURAL MOHAIR

After 1 hour of cooking, the water should be clear and the colors of the mohair blended.

Shawl, *knitted by Bernice Herron, Huntington Beach, California, 2011.*
Fiber artists of all kinds can find wonderfully creative ways to use beautiful hand-dyed fleece.

DYEING WITH COMMERCIAL ACID DYE

Dyeing Nylon

batch 15

RESULT: PC #733 IVY, #724 KEY LIME, AND #808 RASPBERRY OVER NYLON LOOPS

Nylon potholder loops overdyed with PC #733 Ivy, #724 Key Lime, and #808 Raspberry.

▲▲▲

Easy to dye and easy to carry around, this found fiber may be just what you need for your next project.

▲▲▲

Ways to Use Dyed Nylon

▲ Hooking projects
▲ Sculpted features
▲ Interesting fringe

Rug hookers have always scouted around for anything that could be used to make a rug, so it is no surprise that the more substantial nylons of long ago were used for that purpose. When cut and pulled, relatively wide pieces of nylon fabric curl up on the sides to make a strip that has a unique look when hooked. It is, in fact, a look that I really like. However, as it is a bit hard to find and, in my opinion, irritating to hand cut, nylon was not a fiber that I sought out for hooking.

That all changed one day when it suddenly dawned on me that most of the old pot holder loops from my childhood craft days were made out of nylon. Not only are nylon craft pot holder loops readily available and fairly cheap, they come cut in useable widths. You don't need anything more expensive than a pair of scissors to make the initial cut; just stretch them as long as they will tolerate, and snip. Sure, the widths of each strip are all a little different, but I really like the antique look of all those various strip sizes when they are hooked together.

Nylon is a great fiber to use when teaching children how to hook. The loops can be used straight from the bag, without the need for an expensive cutter system to prep them, so the process is very kid-friendly. For all the same reasons, nylon craft loops are also a natural for people who want to hook projects on the go without the burden of packing a lot of equipment. Unlike many of our cutting machines, nylon loops appear innocent enough to airport security.

Carnival Paws, *15" x 11", overdyed nylon pot holder loops/strips in various factory widths on primitive linen. Designed and hooked by Gene Shepherd, Anaheim, California, 2012.*

 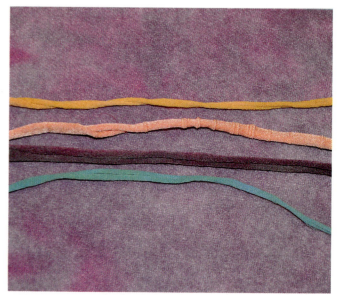

Nylon strips seem flat and unusable for hooking until the loop is cut at one spot and the entire piece is vigorously stretched. Such aggressive behavior turns the seemingly gossamer strips into tight little cords that hook up very well.

And why limit yourself to one color family when it is almost as easy to produce three or four at the same time?

Sure. If you want, you could use nylon craft loops as is. But why stop with as-is when commercial dyes will work with nylon?

Just as various colors of wool fabric were blended into a new color family (batch 3: Overdyeing Colored Wool) with a bath in a single color of dye, so too can the neon colors of the nylon loops be tamed and unified. You'll have some standout loops in every batch; however, even the standout loops will blend in and harmonize with the rest of the repurposed loops.

Nylon Dyeing Cheat Sheet

The Instructions That Do Not Change

- Use commercial dye mixed in boiling water.
- Use citric acid or vinegar to set.
- Cook the nylon at a simmer for 1 hour.

The Instructions That Do Change

- Because of the small fiber pieces being used, choose smaller cooking vessels. Small, shallow pans or glass jars are ideal.
- While the length and temperature of the cook time is important, choose a cooking method that is more gentle than a rough boil on top of the stove. After the initial application of dye, either oven bake the batch or place it in a glass jar and cook it in a water bath to set.
- Presoaking and Synthrapol are optional.

Modified Stacked Pot . . . in a Jar

Step 1: Mix up three and no more than four colors of dye, $1/32$ to $1/16$ tsp. each, in 1 cup boiling water. Add $1/4$ tsp. citric acid to each color and set the colors aside.

Step 2: Put a handful of nylon craft loops into a glass, quart-sized jar. They do not need to be presoaked. Push them down as best you can, then dump in the first color of mixed dye solution.

Step 3: Use a long spoon or tongs to push all the loops under the dye solution. It is amazing how quickly the nylon will take up the hot liquid even though the jar is not on a heat source.

Step 5: Pour in the second color of mixed dye. Tamp all the new loops down into the dye mixture. While I do not stir these two layers of loops, I often wiggle them, just a bit, to ensure a little mingling of dye at the layers. Wiggling may not make much difference, but I think it does, so I feel better doing it.

My favorite container is a recycled sweet pickle jar. It really comes in handy when dyeing sweet colors like PC #808 Raspberry, PC #719 Grasshopper, and PC #733 Ivy. Of course, when nylons with a bit more bite need to be dyed, I go with a dill pickle jar and edgier colors.

Step 4: Put another handful of nylon loops into the jar and tamp them down. Some of the new loops will interact with the first dye solution; the upper portion will not.

Step 6: Add layers three and four in the same way. The number of layers you can fit depends on the size of the jar and the handfuls of loops being added at each level. Stop adding dye and loops when the jar gets full.

Top off the jar with enough boiling water to fill it, then cover the container with clear plastic film. Place the jar on a rack in a simmering water bath for 1 hour. I watch the jars while they cook to make sure they stay upright and full of water.

Regardless of the technique you use to dye nylon craft strips, be most careful with them after they come out of their jar or pan. Just like the angler who does not set the hook, I have a propensity for allowing nylon strips to get away—and go down the drain—before I can get them landed.

To trap those slippery worms, I always pour the pan or jar of dyed nylon strips into a large colander. In the safety of a colander, they can then be plunged and rinsed in two different clear baths. Since moving to this procedure, I have not lost any strips.

Finished strips are also a bit difficult to dry. To speed that process, I use handy manual drying methods. (These methods can also be used for mohair.)

Technique number one calls for all the wet strips to go immediately from the colander into any kitchen towel.

Adapting Other Techniques

When you need more control in a dye technique, use a shallow stainless steel pan instead of a jar. Any general spot dye, a graduated spot, or dump dye, would work better in a pan. This is a good method for antique black.

◢ Preheat your oven to 250°F.

◢ Mix up whichever colors of dye you need for this process.

This antique black background was made in a shallow stainless steel pan. Although the amount of dry dye is dependent on the amount of fiber being colored, for this particular batch, I prepared four separate colors each in 1 cup boiling water: 1/4 tsp. PC #672 Jet Black, 1/8 tsp. each PC #819 Purple, PC #733 Ivy, and PC #122 Mustard.

◢ Put enough nylon loops in the shallow pan to make a 1 inch-thick layer.

◢ Add water to the pan so that it just comes to the top of the nylon.

◢ Add a little citric acid to the pan. Place the pan on a stove and turn on the heat.

◢ Once the water comes to a boil, start spotting the nylon. Begin with black, making even spots over the entire surface. Use approximately half of the black, then set it aside. Push the loops under the water level, but avoid stirring the pan. There should be some untouched spots throughout the pan. The black dye will go into the nylon in short order.

◢ Once the water is fairly clear, spot the nylon with each of the other colors, giving the color time, with each application, to go into the nylon. As these colors are added, gently rearrange the nylon so that all parts of the fiber can come in contact with the dye. You may not wish to add all of these colors at this time.

◢ The dye should absorb fairly fast. Check the nylon to make sure it is as dark as you want. Using the remainder of the mixed black, re-spot the nylon wherever necessary. The goal is to make black fiber with highlights of purple, green, and gold. Because the nylon started out in a wild array of neon colors, there will already be some natural highlights. This last addition of black is simply a means of leveling out the excess color. As soon as the fiber looks the way you want, cover the pan with a lid and place it in a 250°F preheated oven to cook for 1 hour.

By twisting each end of the dish towel in an opposite direction, all those little strips can be, in effect, wrung out. The thicker the towel, the more absorption takes place. This procedure, which does work effectively, is rather hard on the hands and wrists of the one doing the twisting.

Once you have removed the excess water, spread the strips out in a well-ventilated, shaded area to dry. A window screen provides better ventilation than a flat surface. As they dry during the course of a day, this arrangement allows for a quick and easy stir, every couple of hours, so that all strips can evenly dry.

Like their wool counterparts, unneeded nylon strips can be stored indefinitely in your stash.

Way number two, becoming a human salad spinner, is a bit more fun and a lot more messy, which may be why this is my favorite method. Still, I highly recommend it. This version calls for all the wet, rinsed strips to go directly into a thin cloth tea towel. Collect the sides into a bundle and tie securely, then take the package outside. As a person who made his vocal debut at the age of five singing "Only a Boy Named David," it stands to reason that I choose to recreate that memorable musical moment while swinging the wet bag of nylon around my head, like David did when meeting Goliath, and singing the chorus of said song at the top of my lungs. As the bag goes round and round, not only do I efficiently get the rinse water out of the nylons, but I also water a large section of my yard.

| TIP | **LIGHT COLORS** |

When you want pure, light colored strips of any color, pick out the white strips from the bag for a special batch. Just as white wool is a good vehicle for pure colors, so are white nylon loops.

DYEING WITHOUT DYE

Bleeding Wool

batch 16

This rainbow of color was made by bleeding an odd assortment of found wool in the three primary colors.

▲▲▲

Offered free wool? Never turn it down. With one of these bleeds you can always find a way to tweak it to your liking.

▲▲▲

The mixed-color-bleed stash of wool above was created by bleeding the primary color pieces of the fabric. No dry dye was added to the three different baths used to create them. This grouping proves that, with a careful, selective bleed, anyone can use pieces of wool from their existing stash to make a wide variety of beautiful colors without ever buying any commercial dyes.

Regardless of how hard we work to set a batch of dyed wool, if it encounters the right circumstances that dye will begin to bleed out of the fabric. That is why we don't shampoo hooked rugs with hot water. The trick to bleeding wool is to get it to bleed on our terms. Keep these rules in mind when bleeding wool:

◢ Hot water and a softening agent will cause dyed wool to bleed.

◢ If dyed wool bleeds where there is a lot of water and a lot of agitation or stirring, the color will do a lot of moving.

◢ If dyed wool bleeds where there is limited water and limited or no agitation, the color will not move around very much.

◢ Pick the right time to stop the color movement.

How to Use Bled Wool

◢ Marry two or more colors
◢ Tone down wild pieces
◢ As a source of dye for other pieces

Bleeding Wool 145

Welcome, 34" x 28", #4-, 5-, 6-, and 8-cut overdyed vintage wool on Scottish burlap. Designed by Edward Sands Frost; hooked by Teresa Heinze, Lubbock, Texas, 2012.

This rug was hooked for the Hooked Rug Museum of North America. The Bled Red batch shown in this section was made specifically for the flowers in Teresa's re-creation of this historic rug pattern. To get into the spirit of this project, I used mostly found wool that I had inherited from deceased fiber artists. Many of the pieces came from garments that appeared to be older than I am! Still, having been preserved with care until needed, they were quite capable of being pressed into service. The leaves and stems were made using the stacked pot method (batch 12), and the background was created as an Antique Black variation, which will be described in batch 17. Photo by Naomi Hill

Version 1: Bled Red

Let's say you want a red background for your next hooked project but don't have enough of any one piece of wool to use for the entire piece. However, you do have a lot of odd little pieces of found wool fabric in a vast variety of cherry red, fire engine red, orange red, rose, pink, and coral in all sorts of light and dark variations.

Here's your solution: Put all of the reds in a pot of simmering water with a bit of Synthrapol or some other softening agent. As the combination of boiling water, Synthrapol, and your stirring do their job, all of the different red dyes will come out into the water, making a new shade of red.

TIP — USING FOUND WOOL

When prepping found pieces for a bleed, I do not reconfigure them into regular yardage sizes like I do with new wool. (I do remove zippers, buttons, lining, and so on.) All irregular shapes are welcome, as the odd edges will add just that much more color to the bath. Even bad wool that will be useless to hook is valuable to a pot if it is a bleeder!

mixture back into the pot while stirring to see how much that affects the coloration. Add more if you want a darker color. Any leftover mixed dye can go in the fridge to be saved for another project.

After the proper color bath has been achieved, add either citric acid crystals or white vinegar to the pot and set your cooking timer for 1 hour. Stir every so often to achieve a more uniform look. Stir less often if you want mottling.

When making this demonstration batch, I went with the red bath that my pieces naturally created with their bleed. The end result was a collection of toned down, married reds that worked together when hooked. Since some of the pieces started out very dark and others very light, the finished pieces still retained some differences in value.

However, the finished pieces look related, and the lights and darks complement each other instead of competing for attention.

What I did with this group of non-related reds can easily be done with other color family groups. A bunch of different greens thrown together in a bleed-and-set dye bath will marry to make a new group of related greens. The same will happen with batches of any color group.

In no time at all, a dip of water from the newly created dye bath will indicate the color direction the pot is beginning to take. If nothing else is done other than to force a good bleed before setting the wool again, the resultant pieces will "marry" to produce a collection of new reds that go together. While bleeding unifies the various pieces that come out of the pot, it also usually tones down those colors.

However, should you look at this new red color bath and not find it to your satisfaction—perhaps you want it darker—you still have an opportunity to change the coloration. (Note: Wet wool always looks darker than it does when it dries, so take that into account before tweaking any mix.)

- Add some more dark red wool and let it bleed into the mix, thereby darkening the mixture.

- Add a small piece of dark green wool and stir vigorously as it bleeds into the mix. Green is opposite red on the standard color wheel, so the green will darken the red. If you try this, add a little piece at a time until you get the right coloration. Adding more is much easier than taking it back out!

- Nudge your dye bath in whatever direction you want it to go with just a little bit of commercial mixed dye. On a big pot like this, start with $^1/_{16}$ tsp. of dye at a time. Dip out some of the red dye bath to mix the dye in a measuring cup, then pour half of the

Welcome (detail). I did not stir the pot much after adding the citric acid, and with careful scrutiny, you can pick out places where some of the darker, purplish reds created some dark mottling on their next door neighbor in the dye pot. I personally prefer such accents as I think they make the end result more interesting. **Photo by Naomi Hill**

Version 2: Selective Mixed Color Bleed

While all of that information provides a useful tool in our artistic arsenal, things get much more interesting when color groups are mixed.

Step 1: For an interesting experiment, dig through your stash of wool to make piles of yellow, red, and blue pieces. Select pure versions of these colors in any light to dark values you can find.

As discussed in batch 8 (Your own Wheel of Color), different-colored dye solutions change when they come in contact with other colors. The same is true when bleeding pieces of colored wool.

Step 2: Rearrange the stacks of dry wool so that each of the three groups gets mixed with the other two. This should produce three new groups of pieces: red/yellow, yellow/blue, and red/blue.

Step 3: Bring three pots of water to a boil, and add a little Synthrapol or Jet Dry to the water. The combination of heat and softening agent will release the dye in the wool.

Controlling the Shift

Based on our experiments in other sections of this book, we know the following:

▲ Red and yellow will produce orange.

▲ Yellow and blue will produce green.

▲ Red and blue will produce purple.

While it seems that all colors are equal, pragmatically speaking, red and blue tend to be bleeding bullies that, when left unchecked, will overpower yellow. That is fine if you want a very red red/orange and a very blue blue/green. If you want greater variety in the orange and green pots, then you'll need to add extra yellow wool to both stacks. More yellow wool—probably double the amount of the others—will spread out the two stronger colors, allowing for greater variation.

When it comes to the battle for dominance in the red/blue pot, it all depends on the amount of color in the particular pieces of red and blue you chose. For variation in those pots, add some pinks and baby blues to the stack.

Step 4: Orange Pot—Add all the red wool to the first pot. You do not need to soak this wool as the simmering bath will quickly trigger the release of red dye. Stirring will help. Allow the pot to cook for about 4 or 5 minutes to ensure a good red bleed. Do not add citric acid or vinegar right now.

Step 5: For maximum variation in the orange pot, stagger the addition of yellow wool, like the system used for the Lazy Swatch in batch 4. As one never knows exactly how much yellow will be needed—because the amount of red dye in the wool cannot be measured ahead of time—I suggest having extra pieces of yellow at the ready.

It is not necessary to presoak this wool before adding it to the pot. If you are putting in twice as much yellow as red, start by dropping in about one-fourth of the yellow pieces. Once in the pot, stir to keep the yellow pieces moving so that they come in contact with the red bath. Even though your eye may not see it yet, yellow will have started moving into the bath within the first few moments of insertion. Wait 60 to 90 seconds, and drop in a second batch of yellow, continuing to stir. After another 60 seconds, add 1 Tbsp. of citric acid and the third batch of yellow wool. Continue to stir.

If the pot has great variation at this point, stop adding yellow pieces and set the timer for 1 hour of cooking. However, red dye baths are rather deceptive and they often continue to color wool even when the water appears to be fairly clear. To be safe, after another 60 seconds or so, add that final batch of yellow pieces. Chances are they will be needed to soak up the final bits of red. Once everything is in, cover the pot and cook at a simmer for 1 hour.

Step 6: Green Pot—Add all the dark blues to a new pot, and stir to trigger the release of the fabric's dye. After allowing the blues to cook and bleed for about 4 to 5 minutes, add the yellow wool in the same basic staggered procedure as described in step 5. If you have some very light blue pieces of wool, add them with the second or third batch of yellow pieces. Once a good gradation is reached, cover the pot and cook the wool for 1 hour to set.

Step 7: Purple Pot—In the third pot of water, add the dark blues and the dark reds at the same time and let them slug it out for dominance. If you are rooting for the red/purple team and think that blue is getting an upper hand, add some more red until you like the result. If team blue/violet is your favorite, ensure that goal by tipping the coloration of the pot with another piece or two of blue. After 4 to 5 minutes, begin staggering the addition of light pinks and blues, along with some citric acid. Once the water begins to clear, cover and cook on simmer for 1 hour.

Wool Yarn Bleeds Too

Bleed 1

What works with dyed wool fabric also works with dyed wool yarn. If yellow and blue hanks of yarn are placed in a pot of boiling water and cooked until they bleed, new colors will be created in the process.

Since equal amounts of the two colors were used, the stronger blue turned the yellow into a blue-green yarn.

Bleed 2

Why not mix wool yarn and wool fabric in one bath? In this case, additional yellow fabric was called in to dilute the strength of the bleeding blue yarn. It was added in the method described in the Selective Mixed Color Bleed.

The addition of more yellow fabric produced lighter greens with greater variation.

Even the strong blue wool was affected with this bleed.

Version 3: Multicolor Bleed

If you had success with the Selective Color Bleed, you might be tempted to just start throwing piles of wool in a pot, assuming that any combination of colored wool pieces could be magically transformed with the addition of boiling water, a wetting agent, citric acid, and 1 hour of cooking time. However, once wool from all three of the primary colors is allowed to bleed together, the process usually ends up producing a gray to brown murky bath that tones down or dulls all the wool. If you want subdued colors this all-color bleed is a useful and quick way of creating just such a stash.

Step 1: Select a good mixture of wool fabric that has fairly equal amounts of all three primary colors: red, yellow, and blue.

Step 2: Even before the water comes to a boil, place all the wool in the pot, along with some Synthrapol. The water level needs to be 2 or 3 inches higher than the space taken by the wool. Extra water will allow the newly released dye to travel freely into a place where it can mix with its colorful neighbors. As the pot heats up, stir frequently to encourage this process. A short boil (before adding citric acid) will release

less dye than a long boil. If just a little toning down is required, boil the wool for 2 to 3 minutes (or when your eye can tell that there is a lot of color in the water) and add the citric acid. If you want a lot of change, cook the wool for 6 to 10 minutes before stopping the process with the addition of citric acid crystals; cook for another 60 minutes to set the wool.

The pieces from this pot were cooked at a boil for about 5 minutes before the citric acid was added. They took on a decided reddish brown hue because I put more red pieces in the mix than blue. More blue pieces would have pushed the end product toward gray instead of brown. By adding in the right colored mix of pieces at the beginning, or even as a color adjustment while the pot boils, you can push the color in whichever direction you choose.

Wool selvedges were used for this particular batch and chosen in a highly scientific way: I closed my eyes and grabbed as much as I could in my two hands. The process would work just as well with colored pieces of wool fabric.

Version 4: Restricted Multicolored Bleed

If they are restricted in their flow, colors can bleed out and still retain most of their personality. In the same way that we keep a feisty dog on a leash, so too can colors be restricted, or held back, from interaction with other colors. Here are two ways to rein in a bleed.

Cut Worm Bleed

Step 1: Choose two different pieces of host wool fabric that are the same size. One light and one dark make for a good combination. I used 1/4-yard pieces of Dorr Marigold and Mango. Nothing needs to be presoaked for this process.

Step 2: Place the lighter piece of fabric on a worktable. Cover it loosely with a selection of cut wool strips from your leftover worm storage bin. While any colors could be used, this particular batch had light to dark greens, teals, and various blue worms.

Step 3: Place the darker piece of wool on top of the first two layers.

Step 4: Carefully roll the three layers, make a twist, and secure it with strong string. (See steps 3 to 5 in batch 18: Marbleized Wool.) It is important to roll and twist as tightly as possible: a tight twist restricts dye movement once the bleeding process begins.

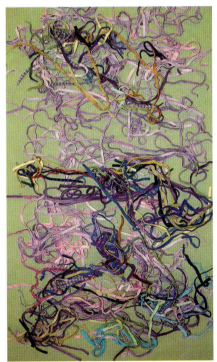

Most pots have room for two twists, so take advantage of the boiling water, Synthrapol, citric acid, and cook time by making a second twist. Yes, two can cook for the price of one. I twisted strips of teal, navy, various medium blues, gold, yellow, and purple between layers of Dorr Sunflower and #101 (Medium Green). I rolled it so the light yellow ended up on the outside of the twist.

When cooking two twists together, it is a good idea to have two outside colors that are similar so that one twist does not contaminate the other during the bleeding. Always put the darker color of wool on the inside, which makes it much easier to gauge the progress of the bleed.

Step 5: Add enough water to cover the twists, then add a little Synthrapol. Although every color combination is different, it will probably take a good 10 minutes of cooking before the darker colors really show up on the outside of the twist. When a good bleed has been achieved, add some citric acid and continue cooking for another hour to set. Be sure to add water throughout the entire cook time to keep the twists covered.

Bleeding Wool 151

Had the strips been laid on the wool in a pan of simmering water, all of the dye would have run together, making one of those murky stews. By restricting the flow of the dye with a tight twist, the individual colors of the cut pieces are kept in place, resulting in little bursts of pure color.

> **TIP** **SOGGY WORMS**
>
> To dry the cut worms after the bleed is over, follow the suggestions given for drying nylon strips in batch 15 (see pages 143–144).

Why Use a Cut Worm Bleed?

- Most rug hookers have a boatload of cut worms lying around that never seem to get used. This process at least gives them a way to earn their keep while waiting for a home. Because the worms are so restricted during this bleed, they aren't agitated or raveled out of shape. They can show up, give some dye, and go back into the bin.

- Why make the worms wait? Take a close look at our newly repurposed worms and wool. What do their new colors suggest? From the first twist, the orange wool would make a fantastic hooked or prodded flower, which could be set off by leaves, hooked from the green strips. From the other twist, the purple strips could become a flower. The soft green fabric could be a hooked background. As these two sets of wool have been married, they deserve to stay together.

- When cut and hooked as a background, most of the markings on the fabric will turn into soft flecks or highlights of color, a nice touch in a delicate background. Consequently, after hooking all the motifs in a rug, leftover strips can bring all the colors of the rug into the background.

- Instead of using this method with leftovers, why not use this method to make both the background and all the cut strips needed for a rug? Pick the colors for the rug, cut all the strips, make the controlled bleed for the background, then use the strips to hook the central motifs.

- There is something lovely about the delicate coloration that happens with this technique. It can't be replicated in any other process. For that reason, the wrapping fabric could be left whole and used for appliqué projects or the back side of a pillow—or any place that calls for lovely wool.

Selvedge Bleed for a Scarf

Although similar in appearance to wool created with the jelly roll technique described in batch 7, this process is much easier and quicker. All you need are a 2-yard length of host wool and a bunch of colorful wool selvedges or $1/2$-inch-wide strips. This is a restrictive bleed that brings out the big colorful dog yet keeps it under control and on its leash.

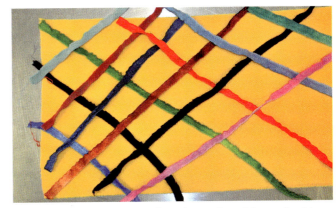

Step 3: Lay the dry piece of wool on a flat table, preferably one that is 6 feet long. Arrange a pattern with the strips of selvedges. You need to have a general plan, but it doesn't need to be too fussy of a plan. Lines do not have to be rigidly measured and pinned down to stay in place. If a pattern line in blue stops in midscarf, cover the end with 1 or 2 inches of a similar piece and continue the design. On the beginning, narrow edge, the strips need to stop right at that edge. On the long sides, they can stick out past the host wool.

Once you get the technique down, the actual layout can be adapted any way you wish.

Step 1: Tear a 2-yard length (by the selvedge) of wool. I used Dorr's Marigold for this particular example. After you measure and tear the length, fold the top width of the wool into four sections as you would to prep a yard of wool for dyeing. Remember to make allowances for the selvedges, as they will eventually be removed. Notch $1/4$ yard sections across the top of the wool as you would for a single yard of wool. Tear at the first notch, creating a piece of wool that is approximately $14 1/4$" wide x 72" long. This creates a skinny, $1/2$-yard piece of wool. Tear the remainder of the wool to make other scarves or divide it into $1/4$ yard sections for your next regular dye session.

Step 2: Collect a colorful pile of hand-torn wool selvedges or wool fabric strips that measure approximately $1/2$ inch wide.

Step 4: After making about 20 inches of your pattern, carefully fold over the narrow end of the wool to hold the edge pieces in place. Then make a roll as tight and straight as possible. As the roll progresses, the selvedges will crinkle and buckle a bit. Every so often, the pattern will need to be smoothed out and tweaked, which is why I don't suggest laying out the entire pattern before you roll it. If you are working on a short table, roll a bit then gently pull back the entire piece to give yourself more room to work. When you adjust the pattern, place a book or some other small weight on the roll so it cannot come undone.

Bleeding Wool 153

The pattern should extend beyond the length of the wool so that color will come out to the very edge.

Step 5: Before the final roll is finished, place a natural-colored 1/8-yard piece of wool next to the raw edge of the scarf. This piece of wool will protect the pattern from being altered during the cooking process. Without it, several inches on the bottom of this end would end up with a muddy coloration.

Step 6: Keep rolling until the entire piece of natural wool is wrapped around the yellow wool. Trim the selvedges that stick out so they can become tie strings to secure the package. Tie the bundle snugly at each end and at two or three places in the middle. All the pieces sticking out the sides can be left to season the pot.

Step 7: Place the entire bundle in a kettle of boiling water with a bit of Synthrapol. This roll has so many layers, the piece will need to cook for at least 15 minutes to get a good bleed. When that moment arrives, add citric acid and cook the wool until set. Because this piece is so thick, I recommend a longer cooking set time of 75 minutes.

This method produces interesting wool because the colors were not allowed to bleed into an indistinct muddle. There is some mingling of color where strips interacted, as well as additional rows of secondary bleeding that made it through two layers of fabric.

The selvedges also come out of the experience changed due to their marriage with the strong Marigold fabric.

Even the natural pieces used simply to shield the end of the roll have interesting colors. If they are not suitable as is, use them as a base in your next spot dye project.

Whether open or restrictive, the bleeding of two or more colors of wool gives an artist amazing opportunities to dye—without ever buying any dye at all!

DYEING WITHOUT DYE

batch 17

Antique Black

RESULT: PC #672 BLACK, #733 IVY, AND #122 MUSTARD OVER NATURAL, MINT, AND SUNFLOWER WOOL

▲▲▲
This way or that way or your own way—whichever way doesn't matter. The end result is still a go-to for antique-style backgrounds.
▲▲▲

Ways to Use Antique Black

- Striking backgrounds
- Interesting wool for black animals
- Great way to recycle found wool

Ask ten rug hookers to define the dye technique called "Antique Black" and you are bound to get at least twelve answers: *It's black, black over multiple colors, green so dark it looks black, black with some gold, black with some green, black with some red* . . . Although I added it here in the Dyeing without Dye section of this book, the technique really does best when made with both a bleed from dark wool and a nudge from some extra dye. I've provided options with and without dye so you can pick the method you like.

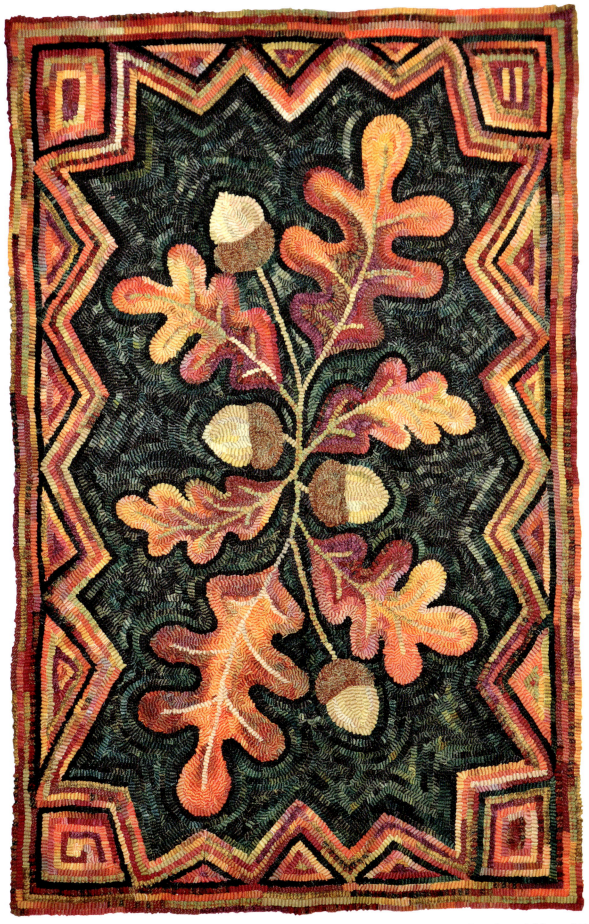

Wm. Pickering Oak Rug, *24" x 36", #6- and 8-cut wool on primitive linen. Designed and hooked by Gene Shepherd, Anaheim, California, 2011. The background for this rug was made with Antique Black over new wool.*

Version 1: All-Dark Bleed

As a nod to the past, gather approximately 1 yard of dark material from your stash of vintage wool. At least two-thirds to three-quarters of the pieces need to be black. To complete the 1-yard (³⁄4 pound of wool) total pile, choose a mixture of dark pieces from these families: brown, purple, gray, charcoal, navy, green, and red. Place them all in a pot with plenty of water and some Synthrapol. Boil the pot for approximately 15 to 20 minutes to ensure a good bleed. Add citric acid and continue to cook the wool for 1 hour to set it. Stir frequently during the entire process.

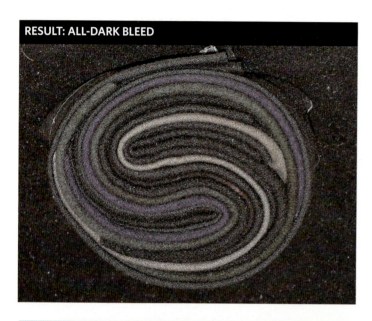
RESULT: ALL-DARK BLEED

Even though the black wool had enough internal dye to go solo on its mission to change its pot mates, the changes are fairly subtle and not quite bold enough to suit my tastes. However, if your goal is a subtle blending, this would be an easy way to achieve it.

Version 2: Dark Bleed with Light

In this version of Antique Black, instead of having a ratio of triple black pieces to a smaller ensemble of mixed-color wool, make the ratio 6 black to 1 light bright.

Gather approximately 1½ yards of various black pieces and about ¼ yard of bright, mixed-color pieces. Follow the same cooking directions given in version 1 for this pot.

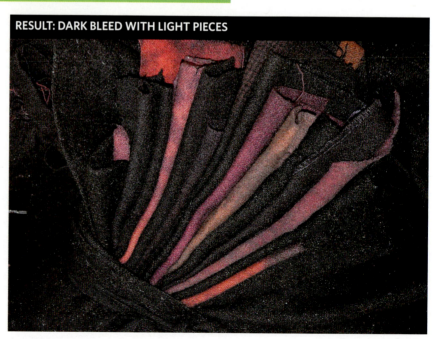
RESULT: DARK BLEED WITH LIGHT PIECES

Enough black bleed was present in version 2 to significantly darken the brighter pieces. Still, when finished, they don't exactly blend in.

Version 3: Black Wool Bleed Plus Black Dye

Step 1: Instead of using irregular pieces of found wool, this version is made with new wool. To make it, assemble ¾ yard of black wool and ¼-yard pieces each of a strong yellow (Dorr Marigold), red (Dorr Crimson), purple, brown (Dorr #7), and teal. Note: Any colored wool close to these colors will work.

Step 2: Place all the wool in a large kettle of boiling water and Synthrapol. Allow the wool to cook and bleed out for about 10 to 12 minutes. Stir the wool often.

Step 3: Measure ½ tsp. of any good commercial black dye into a mixing cup. Fill the cup with boiling water, and stir well until mixed. Pour the black dye into the pot. Continue stirring the simmering wool for a couple more minutes, and then add citric acid. If the pot is stirred frequently after the addition of the citric acid, the dyed pieces will have less mottling. Less mottling, in this case, means darker variations of wool.

Because this batch was stirred frequently, the resultant pieces of wool are not glaringly different. They will go nicely together in a hooked background.

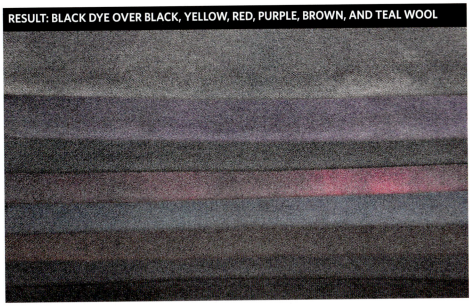

RESULT: BLACK DYE OVER BLACK, YELLOW, RED, PURPLE, BROWN, AND TEAL WOOL

Version 4: Dyeing Antique Black over a Stash

Since Antique Black is a traditional, time-honored approach for making background wool, this method was used to recreate two historic Frost rug designs made for the Hooked Rug Museum of North America.

Step 1: Assemble 2 yards (1½ lbs.) of mixed-color and black wool pieces. Place them in a large steamer pan of water and Synthrapol. Turn on the heat and bring the water to a boil.

If desired, add enough wool yarn to whip the edge of a standard-sized rug.

Step 2: Use four individual measuring cups to mix the four separate colors (¾ tsp. dye each): PC #819 Purple, PC #122 Mustard, PC #733 Ivy and PC #672 Black. Stir each color until the dye is completely dissolved. Add ½ tsp. citric acid to each cup, and stir again.

Step 3: Transfer the black dye to a 2-quart saucepan. Rinse out the measuring cup with water, and pour the rinse water into the saucepan. Add enough additional water to make a black bath of about four cups.

Step 4: After the pan of wool comes to a good boil, pour out 2½ to 3 cups of the mixed black dye to spot six or seven locations in the pan. Reserve the rest for later. Let the bath cook for a minute, then stick a pair of tongs into the center of each spot and wiggle a bit to gently help disperse the black dye.

Step 5: Immediately pour the purple dye into the saucepan, then rinse the measuring cup out with hot water and add it to the saucepan as in step 3. Add more water, and start spotting the cooking wool in places that did not receive any of the black. Once added, do the tong wiggle.

Step 6: Before adding another color of dye, use the tongs to reposition the wool so that new, uncolored peaks of wool come to the surface.

Step 7: Pour the Ivy dye into the saucepan and remix as before. Spot untouched sections of the cooking wool with the Ivy mixture. Do a tong wiggle, along with another repositioning of the wool.

Step 8: Add the Mustard so that any bare spots are covered. Do a fairly aggressive repositioning of the wool to make sure there are no missed areas. Punch the wool under the bath.

TIP — THE TONG WIGGLE

The "tong wiggle" is a technique worth learning. No agitation in the pan will allow the dye to stay where it was put. Too much agitation will force the separate colors to mingle into a muddy mess before leaving their unique color mark. With the practiced flick of the wrist, a good tong wiggle will gently disperse the dye and encourage important rendezvous with other colors.

TIP — THROW IN SOME YARN

When dyeing a special color or batch of wool for a hooking project, always throw in a bit of wool yarn so that you can be ready to whip the finished edge with a perfect match.

At this point in the process, the cooking wool should look like the wool in this photo. If some spots in the wool seem too light, use a measuring cup to quickly check the color of the dye bath. If there is still a good amount of color in the bath, keep pushing the light spots of wool under the surface so more of the dye can be absorbed. Add some of the reserved black dye if the pan needs to go even darker. Since pans of wool usually get darker as they cook, give the process a few more minutes of cook time. If you are satisfied with the wool, cover the pan and cook for 1 hour. If you need more color variation, mix up a little extra dye in whichever colors are needed and do a bit more spotting until satisfied. Do remember that wet wool is always darker than dry wool.

RESULT: PC #819 PURPLE, #122 MUSTARD, #733 IVY, AND #672 BLACK OVER ASSORTED BLACK AND COLORED WOOLS

This selection of black and multicolored wool pieces was made with the recipe as described in version 4: Dyeing Antique Black over a Stash.

RESULT: PC #338 MAGENTA, #122 MUSTARD, #733 IVY, AND #672 BLACK OVER ASSORTED BLACK AND COLORED WOOLS

This adaptation of version 4 differed in only one respect: PC #338 Magenta was used instead of Purple. Taking out the purple and adding the red, gave the end result a more reddish cast. This background was used in a second Frost rug, Welcome #28, hooked by Teresa Heinze.

This example of version 4 used less black dye than the other examples and more of two colors, #733 Ivy and #122 Mustard, over a mixture of new Natural, Sunflower, and Mint wool. After spotting all three colors over the wool, I added an additional bath of Ivy to the pan for the final cook time. Had that final bath been Mustard or Black, it would have taken the pan in a completely different direction. You can push the final product in any way you desire by adding or omitting amounts of black or other colors.

RESULT: PC #672 BLACK, #733 IVY, AND #122 MUSTARD WITH AN IVY WASH OVER ASSORTED COLORED WOOLS

In **Welcome**, *a background with a reddish cast was the better choice since red flowers are the dominant aspect of the artist's interpretation of the historic design. (See the full rug on page 146.)*

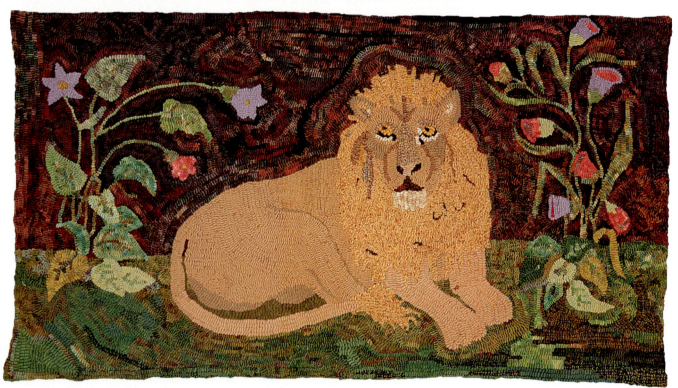

Frost Lion #176, *25" x 46", #8- and 10-cut recycled wool on burlap. Designed by Edward Sands Frost; wool dyed by Gene Shepherd; hooked by Phyllis Lindblade, Hamburg, Michigan, 2012.*

The Frost Lion is one of 10 historic Frost patterns that were recreated by artists from both the United States and Canada for the Hooked Rug Museum of North America. Since fiber artists in the 1800s usually relied on recycled materials for their rug making, recycled wool was dyed for both the Antique Black background (version 4) and all the flowers and vegetation (Stacked Pot Method, batch 12). Photo by Roxane Bay/Let There Be Light Photo Studio

DYEING WITHOUT DYE

Marbleized Wool

batch 18

RESULT: DORR CRIMSON, MARIGOLD, AND SUNFLOWER MARBLEIZED

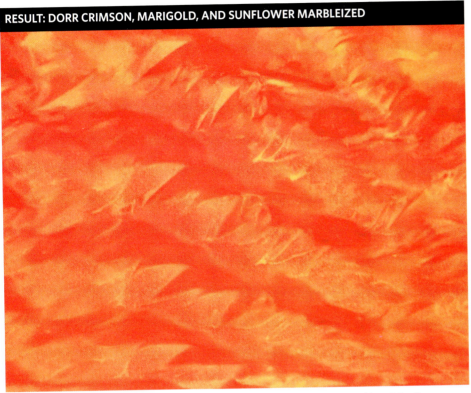

This "Sunflower" marbleized wool was made from a twist of Dorr Crimson, Marigold, and Sunflower.

▲▲▲

Double your efforts with this two-in-one dyeing technique. Marbleizing creates a distinctly different front and back for each piece of wool.

▲▲▲

The distinctive patterning of marbleized wool suggested this method's name. Marbleized wool is produced when three pieces of colored wool are jelly-rolled, twisted, cooked until bled, and then set. For this procedure, I only use off-the-bolt colored wool directly as it comes from the manufacturer. I never get the same results from hand-dyed wool.

Ways to Use Marbleized Wool

▲ Substitute for textured wool

▲ Great backgrounds

▲ Vegetation and flowers

▲ Landscapes

▲ Absolutely everything

Each piece of marbleized wool, because it lies between two different pieces of wool while cooking, ends up with a different coloration on each side of every piece. Therefore, three pieces of wool being dyed in this fashion will really produce six distinctive colors and patterns of finished wool. Because the three pieces put into the pot have all bled on each other, their colors have been "married," resulting in wool that goes together.

Fowl Mood, *14" square, #8-cut wool on primitive linen. Designed and hooked by Gene Shepherd, Anaheim, California, 2009.*

The blue and green background colors used in this piece were made in the same twist of marbleized wool.

That 2-in-1 option comes in handy when you need a little shadow in the background or the motif. Simply ignore the right/wrong side of the strip rules and go for the color that suits your purposes.

Step 1: Choose three 1/4-yard (approximately 18 by 30 inches) pieces of wool—a dark, a medium, and a light color—that are the same size and will make a nice blend. When choosing wool, remember that some colors are prodigious givers and some are takers; you need a mixture of both to make a good blend. You'll need a bit of good string.

Step 2: While there is no right or wrong way to position the pieces, I prefer this order: light wool on the bottom, medium in the middle, then dark on the top. Wool used for this process is not presoaked.

Step 3: Starting at the longest edge of the stack, roll the three pieces in a tight jelly-roll fashion. If the wool wants to wrinkle a bit, that is fine. In fact, a bit of scrunching makes the final pattern more interesting.

The three edges of the wool should be fairly close together when the roll is finished. Avoid gaps bigger than 1/4".

Cooking Pointers for Marbleized Wool

▲ Too much water in the pot (covering the twist) will overpromote bleeding. Much of that distinctive marbleized marking will be lost.

▲ Not enough water in the pot (half of the twist or less) will discourage movement of the bleed, which will limit those distinctive markings.

▲ Waiting too long to add citric acid (after the outside wool is totally recolored) will produce pieces without significant markings.

▲ Adding citric acid before a good bleed shows up on the outside wool will stop the bleed before good markings can be set.

▲ While all those pointers may give the impression that this is a finicky technique, nothing could be further from the truth. In reality, marbleizing wool is fairly easy and very forgiving. All you really need is a comfortable pair of shoes and a little patience.

When cut and hooked, marbleized wool often ends up producing an effect that is reminiscent of the way plaids and tweeds look when hooked.

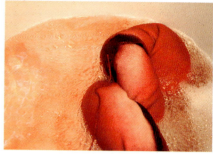

Step 4: Holding one end of the roll in each hand, twist each end of the roll in opposite directions. Make seven or eight complete revolutions so that the roll is now so tight that it wants to twist back on itself. Most beginners make the mistake of stopping too soon. Granted, it is a little tricky to do, but don't give up. Use your hip, table, arm, or a friend to stabilize the twist so that your hand can be repositioned to keep the process going. When you can twist no more, bring the two ends of the twist together.

Step 6: Place the twist in a pot of water. The water should cover about two-thirds of the wool. Add a good squirt of Synthrapol to the water, and turn on the heat.

Step 8: When satisfied with the bleed, add vinegar or citric acid to the pot to stop the bleed and begin the set. Since setting is a process that takes a few minutes, the trick is to add the acid a little before the twist has hit your desired look. The twist will get a little darker as the dye sets. After adding the acid, cover the pot and cook the wool for 1 hour. Check every so often to make sure the water level in the pot stays at a level that covers about two-thirds of the twist.

Step 5: If you do not produce a neat, tight twist like the one shown in this photo, reroll the wool and give it another try. Once the twist is right, secure the two ends with natural cotton string so they cannot unwind.

Step 7: Heat the water to a boil, and allow the wool to cook until it is obvious that the deeper colors are bleeding out into the surface layer of wool. This may take 6 to 10 minutes.

Marbleizing Madness

To take a little of the guesswork out of making marbleized wool, here are 23 combinations made from stock colors produced by Dorr Wool. Similar colors from other suppliers can be used when making these twists. Use them as shown or use these photos for inspiration to make your own versions. For those Dorr colors designated by numbers, I have supplied my descriptive assessment of the color. In each case, the original wool pieces are shown on the left, followed by the six sides of the final product. The suggestions for appropriate places to use each grouping came from comments made by visitors in my studio.

RESULT: WHITE, #8218 (GRAY), MORNING GLORY

Twist 1: *White, #8218 (Gray), and Morning Glory—winter sky, smoke, doves, or snow*

RESULT: #8218 (GRAY), MORNING GLORY, #6372 (DARK BLUE)

Twist 2: *#8218 (Gray), Morning Glory, and #6372 (Dark Blue)—water, dark sky, ocean waves, shadows on houses, roofs*

RESULT: NATURAL, #101 (MEDIUM GREEN), SEAFOAM

Twist 3: *Natural, #101 (Medium Green), and Seafoam—succulents, ocean waves, backgrounds, close hillsides, distant hillsides*

Marbleized Wool 167

RESULT: CORN, #101 (MEDIUM GREEN), SEAFOAM

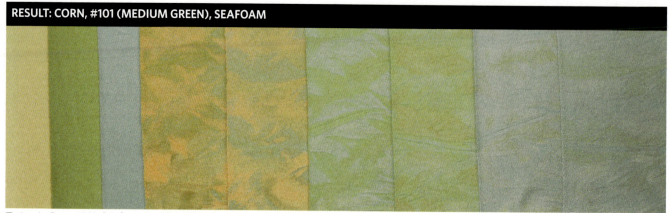

Twist 4: *Corn, #101 (Medium Green), and Seafoam—vegetation, summer grass, blue spruce, backgrounds*

RESULT: LEMONGRASS, CORN, #1042 (ARMY BLANKET GREEN)

Twist 5: *Lemongrass, Corn, and #1042 (Army Blanket Green)—fall grass, military camouflage, leaves*

RESULT: LEMONGRASS, #6372 (MEDIUM BLUE), #102 (MEDIUM GREEN)

Twist 6: *Lemongrass, #6372 (Medium Blue), and #102 (Medium Green)—grass, blue spruce, dark water*

RESULT: LEMONGRASS, MARIGOLD, #6307 (NAVY)

Twist 7: *Lemongrass, Marigold, and #6307 (Navy)—night sky, leaves, evergreens, rock walls, roofs*

RESULT: MARIGOLD, #102 (MEDIUM GREEN), ANTIQUE BLACK

Twist 8: *Marigold, #102 (Medium Green), and Antique Black—leaves, treetops, shadows for vegetation, rooster tail feathers, dusk*

RESULT: NATURAL, CORN, LEMONGRASS

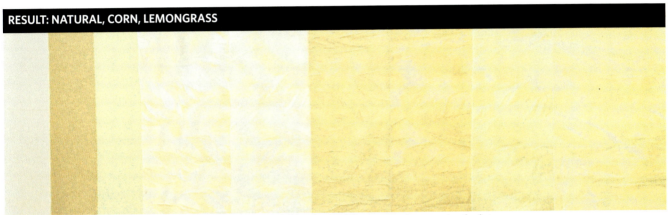

Twist 9: *Natural, Corn, and Lemongrass—ducks, chicks, hay, fodder, shocks, fall grass, sand, mountains, baskets*

RESULT: NATURAL, CORN, MARIGOLD

Twist 10: *Natural, Corn, and Marigold—sun, ducks, chicks, buttercups, cheese, houses*

RESULT: NATURAL, CORN, MANGO

Twist 11: *Natural, Corn, and Mango—pumpkins, dreamsicles, bittersweet, terra cotta roofs, flower pots*

Marbleized Wool

RESULT: SUNFLOWER, MARIGOLD, CRIMSON

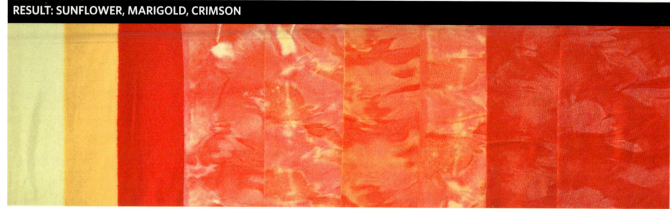

Twist 12: *Sunflower, Marigold, and Crimson—fall leaves, fire, sunsets, barns, tiger lilies*

RESULT: MARIGOLD, CRIMSON, #7268 (MAROON)

Twist 13: *Marigold, Crimson, and #7268 (Maroon)—fall leaves, fire, sunsets, apples, barns, roses, tiger lilies, roosters*

RESULT: WHITE, CRIMSON, #7268 (MAROON)

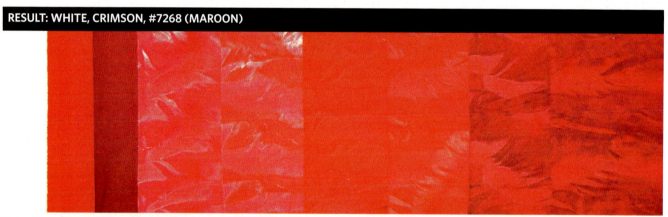

Twist 14: *White, Crimson, and #7268 (Maroon)—apples, cherries, roses, watermelons, roofs, barns*

RESULT: MANGO, #102 (MEDIUM GREEN), AND ANTIQUE RED

Twist 15: *Mango, #102 (Medium Green), and Antique Red—cats, dark horses, fall leaves, tree bark, treetops, mountains*

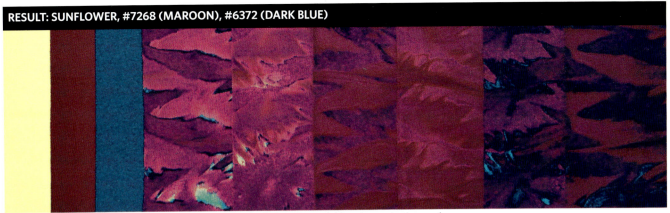

Twist 16: *Sunflower, #7268 (Maroon), and #6372 (Dark Blue)—plums, dahlias, barns, backgrounds*

Twist 17: *Corn, Mango, and #6 (Rich Brown)—tangerines, mud, pumpkins, fall leaves, alley cats, stones, bark, clay pots*

Twist 18: *Marigold, Seafoam, and #7268 (Maroon)—sunset, tiger lilies, little red school house, fire, marigolds, mums, chickens*

Twist 19: *#5 (Medium Brown), Crimson, and Delft—mud, barns, battleships, birds, red rock canyons*

RESULT: MARIGOLD, CRIMSON, #6372 (DARK BLUE)

Twist 20: Marigold, Crimson, and #6372 (Dark Blue)—canyon walls, fall treetops, deep blue sea, sunset

RESULT: MARIGOLD, CRIMSON, ANTIQUE RED

Twist 21: Marigold, Crimson, and Antique Red—Rhode Island Reds, tile roof, painted roses, mums, night sky

RESULT: MARIGOLD, ANTIQUE RED, BLACK

Twist 22: Marigold, Antique Red, and Black—tree bark, stones, distant mountains, backgrounds, lizards, butterflies

RESULT: CORN, #6 (RICH BROWN), ANTIQUE BLACK

Twist 23: Corn, #6 (Rich Brown), and Antique Black—brindle dogs, horses, cats, tree bark, mountains, stones, roofs, mud

If placed between two strong bleeders, even a light gray plaid can be overdyed completely in a marbleized bath. In this case, I put the lighter material in between the crimson and the navy to make sure there was enough color to permeate the fabric.

Marbleized Yarn

Need whipping yarn for a project that features marbleized yarn? It's as simple as one, two, three!

Step 1: Place half a section of yarn over one of the colors of fabric being marbleized. You can use white or natural wool yarn for this process if the host fabrics are big bleeders. However, it works a little better if the yarn color is similar to one of the lighter colors of the fabric used in the twist. The yarn being marbleized here is about half the amount I normally recommend for a large rug. The smaller amount is easier to position on the fabric so that each strand of yarn comes in contact with its host; double the yarn would provide too many layers for good coverage. But you could include an extra, equal amount of yarn in this twist by positioning it next to the top round of wool in the middle, the two groups forming a figure 8 with extra wool extending over the bottom and top edges.

Step 2: Lay a contrasting piece of wool over the first piece of wool and the yarn. Once the second wool is in place, fold the yarn extensions back over the fabric, spreading the yarn so it is not stacked up in layers that cannot receive any dye.

Step 3: With a third piece of wool, on either the bottom or the top of this pile, roll up the wool into a tight twist as described in step 4 of the main marbleizing batch. Cook the wool as described for 1 hour.

Repurpose leftover yarn when you make twists of marbleized wool.

Marbleized Wool 173

Big Momma (detail), 33" x 78", #9- and 10-cut wool on primitive linen. Based on an adaptation of a design by Marny Cardin; hooked by Gene Shepherd, Anaheim, California, 2009.

I keep a big selection of marbleized wool in my personal stash and it finds its way into many of the projects I make. In Big Momma, all the small leaves, orange throats of flowers, and some of the stems are marbleized wool.

China Hen (detail), designed by Gene Shepherd and hooked by Donna Bleam.

The neck and body of this China Hen were hooked with marbleized wool. As is often the case with this technique, hooked sections end up looking as though they were made with textured wool.

Heart of the Home, *24" x 36", #10- and 11-cut wool on primitive linen. Designed and hooked by Gene Shepherd, Anaheim, California, 2008.*
The purple background was made with marbleized wool. With six shades (or sides of wool) from a magenta and purple trio, there were plenty of graduated color and value options to make dark-to-light or light-to-dark progressions. Unfortunately, Dorr no longer makes two of the three pieces used for this twist.

Using nothing but off-bolt colored fabric, the home dyer can make a wonderful rainbow of colors using the marbleizing technique.

Marbleized Wool 175

DYEING WITHOUT DYE

batch **19**

Transitional Pieces

▲▲▲
When you have the time, make a batch of transitional wool so it is ready when you need that something special to bring a little punch to a project.
▲▲▲

Use this process to turn scraps of wool into a wonderful palette of transitional pieces.

Ways to Use Transitional Wool

- Facilitate color transitions in hooking
- Flowers with punch
- Leaves with punch
- Accents
- Outlines
- Repurpose leftover bits
- Backgrounds

This method uses small pieces of previously dyed wool that are overlapped in a pan, where they are soaked, bled, and then re-set during the cooking process. It creates wonderful wool with a split personality when it comes to coloration—no two pieces are ever alike. I call it "transitional wool," as these pieces allow the artist to naturally make a color transition by just hooking the strips in the order in which they were cut.

Double Cross Runner, *12" x 48", #6-cut wool on primitive linen. Traditional geometric design adapted and hooked by Gene Shepherd, Anaheim, California, 2011.*

Historically, this classic design is interpreted with black or dark outlines and a colorful fill. I chose just the opposite approach knowing that this transitional wool outline would shine against a dark fill.

A stack of wool dyed in this fashion has great artistic value as it so often provides just the right spark for an edge, center, or any place that needs a bit of punch. I keep piles of it around for that very reason, as I can never have too much beautiful, interesting wool.

Raid your stash of dyed wool for several small, colorful pieces. Although I typically use about 24 to 30 pieces of uniform size ($1/32$ yard, approximately 3 by 16 inches), smaller amounts of odd pieces can be substituted. To get the maximum effect out of each pan, use a variety of lights, darks, and medium values, with at least one-third of the pieces being "hot" colors. Remember that light pieces will mostly take color and the darker pieces will mostly give color. This wool will not be presoaked.

Step 1: Using a large casserole pan, place one piece of dry wool at the right edge of the pan. With a second piece of a contrasting color, overlap the first piece at its midsection. Repeat this process until the bottom of the pan is covered. I used six pieces of wool to make this first layer, all of them the size of the yellow-green piece on the left.

Transitional Pieces 177

Step 2: Returning to the right side of the pan, make a second layer of wool pieces in exactly the same way. For maximum coloration, avoid layering the same colors on top of each other. While there is no right or wrong way to arrange the colors, give some thought to combinations that will be pleasing. Don't overdo the reds as too many in one pan may overpower the other colors. I usually do four or five layers of wool in each batch.

Step 3: Add Synthrapol to a saucepan of hot tap water and carefully pour it over the dry wool. Do not disturb the layers as you pour.

Step 4: Add more hot water until the wool is barely covered. You need enough water so that the dye, once released in the cooking process, can move from piece to piece but not so much that everything mixes together in a muddy stew. Allow the pan of wool to soak for 5 or 10 minutes without applying any heat.

Step 5: Bring the water to a simmer. The dry wool will soak up some of the water so you may need to add a bit more. When you add water, be careful not to disturb the layers.

Step 6: Allow the wool to cook until the colors start to bleed on each other. Each pan is different, but after 12 to 15 minutes you should see some color transference. I often purposely put one red on the top layer just so I can easily pull back a corner to check the progress. When it is obvious that bleeding is underway, the process can by stopped by adding either citric acid or white vinegar to the pan. *Note:* Vinegar works well in this setting as it can be poured straight from the bottle. If you use citric acid crystals, dissolve a tablespoon in hot water before adding them to the pan.

Step 7: Cover the entire pan with a lid or aluminum foil, and simmer the batch on a low heat for 1 hour until the dye is properly re-set. When you are finished cooking, let the wool cool down before rinsing and drying as usual.

Admire the results. You never really know what this method will produce until the pieces are rinsed and hanging on the line. As with marbleized wool, each side of each piece will be different.

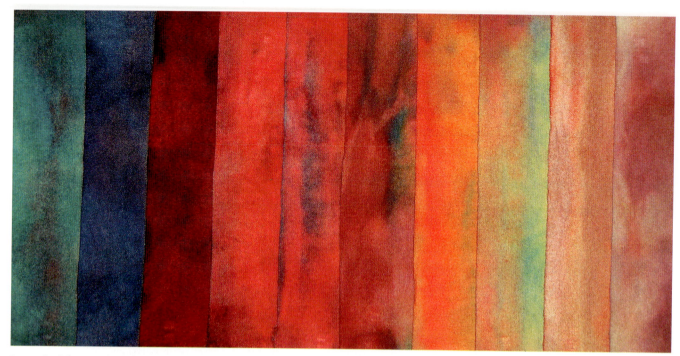

Instead of dyeing wool for a specific project, I dyed this pan of transitional wool with the hope that it would tell me what it was supposed to be. The moment the finished pieces came together on my studio bulletin board, it was as if they spoke in unison: *We are a rooster! Design a pattern for us.*

Fowl Mood (detail), designed and hooked by Gene Shepherd (see the full rug on page 164).

Transitional wool is all about the bleed. The teals, blues, and purples came together to make the body of the rooster. The light and dark reds picked up enough accents to make an interesting comb and wattle. The yellows, golds, reds, and greens mingled to create effective head and neck feathers.

*I used transitional pieces to make the outline in this **Double Cross** geometric (see the full rug on page 177). After hooking three or four strips of a single color, there came a point when a strip of the first color would naturally transition into something different. I added in strips of the new color and hooked until they changed to something else.*

Although I was particular in choosing my cut strips, my pile of transitional pieces included so many natural progressions that I had no trouble finding wool that would do the work for me.

Themed Transitional Wool

While my normal practice is to use a rainbow of colors when making a stash-building pan of transitional wool, "themed" pans, based on the specific needs of a project, are a highly effective way to produce special transitional wool.

That was the case when I needed some "water" wool. I prepped a mixture of white, #44 (antique black green), various bottle greens, medium to dark blues, and purples for a pan that had a water theme. Two-thirds of the pieces chosen were white to medium, with the final choices being a strategic mixture of the darkest colors. This is the before picture (above).

Here is a small selection of the "water" wool after it had cooked and dried.

Possibilities for themed pans of transitional wool:

▲ Water: whites, blues, greens, teals, some purple in various shades

▲ Cherry blossoms: whites, reds, pinks, celery green, gold, brown

▲ Tiger tabby: Black, oranges, browns, yellows, natural

Cherry Blossoms, 21" x 27", #3- and 4-cut wool on linen. Designed, hooked, and prodded by Sarah Province, Silver Spring, Maryland, 2010.

I dyed much of the wool for the prodded sections of Cherry Blossoms using the transitional wool method. Colors chosen for this specific batch were white, various pinks, reds, celery green, gold, and brown. (A few of the blossoms were also hooked with some spot dyes.) Regardless of the wool, it takes the masterful eye of the artist to decide which pieces are right for a particular project and where they should go. By making wool in this fashion, Sarah had plenty of choices with which she could work her magic.
Photo by Phil Province

El Arbol, *36" x 30", #6-cut wool on primitive linen. Designed and hooked by Carla Fortney, Glendale, California, 2012.*
Carla Fortney picked out several of my transitional pieces at a hook-in with the hope that she might find some way to use them. Shortly after getting home, it dawned on her that they would, if put together correctly, make a stunning background for a gnarled tree project that was stalled because she just couldn't find the right wool. She planned the placement of each transitional piece, then cut and hooked the wool to make this stunning background.

INDEX OF TIPS

Accurate cutting lines 14
Animals: Tweaking the
basic process for
more options 114
Bleeding wool:
Controlling the shift 148
Bleeding wool:
Using found wool 146
Bleeding wool:
Why use a cut worm bleed? 152
Bubbling over 44
Color wheel: Downsizing
or supersizing the method 81
Color wheel: Extra dye =
extra stirring 79
Dip dyes: Determining
the length 63
Dip dyes: Hooking tips 67
Dip dyes: Running out of color 68
Dip dyes: The acid moment 67
Dump dye variations 101
Dump dyes: The acid step 101

Dump dyes: The
monster within 104
Extra pot on deck 46
Foam 38
Gene's top 20 colors 23
Hot handles 77
It does not take much
to be related 92
Jelly roll: Downsizing 73
Jelly roll: Remove the pins 72
Jelly roll: Repurposing
the sleeves 73
Leaves: Choosing dye colors 126
Less and more 39
Magic refrigerator dye 95
Marbelized wool:
Cooking pointers 165
Materials for the
essential dye kitchen 2
Mohair: Things to remember
when dyeing 136

Mohair: Two sides 138
Must I cover the dye pot? 28
Nylon dyeing cheat sheet 141
Nylon: Adapting other techniques for nylon 143
Nylon: Light colors 144
Pops of color 41
Rebellious reds 85
Salt dye 130
Selvedges 15
Selvedges: Does the selvedge direction matter? 18
Sheep 35
Spot dye: Selecting colors 93
Spot dyes to suit your every need 98
Spot dyes: Controlling the spots 97
Spot-dyeing multiple unions in one pan: How do I use it? 90
Stir textures more 50
Storing mixed dyes 56
Successful kitchen dyeing 5
Swatches 58
Textures and whites 76
The tong wiggle 160
Transitional pieces: Themed transitional wool 182
Which side is the right side? 87
Whipping yarn: Be prepared to whip 47
Whipping yarn: How much yarn do I need to whip a rug? 21
Whipping yarn: Throw in some yarn 160
Worms 44
Worms: Drying cut worms 152
Yarn: Adapting dye recipes to dye yarn 29
Yarn: Bleeding fabric and yarn together 149
Yarn: Marbelized yarn 173
Yarn: Multitasking in spot dyeing 86

Index and Resources 185

RESOURCES

Geneshepherd.com
Geneshepherd.com is a source of online instruction 24/7, through weekday blogs and a library of over 75 videos. Gene also offers hand-dyed wool, his favorite Pro Chem dyes, Bee Line Dye Spoons, cutters and frames, Dyeing Without Dye kits, plain and off-bolt colored wool, and other dyeing and rug hooking supplies of all kinds.

Rug Hooking Magazine
www.rughookingmagazine.com
Rug Hooking Magazine publishes 5 issues every year packed with stories, trends, how-to articles, patterns, and more, as well as great books on everything rug hooking. To subscribe or order books and back issues, visit our website; also check out our blog and our online magazine, *Rug Beat*.

Dorr Mill
www.dorrmillstore.com
Online store offering wool of all kinds (including many of the colors used the dye batches in this book), as well as dyes, kits, backing, patterns, and other rug hooking supplies.

Also available from *Rug Hooking* Magazine:

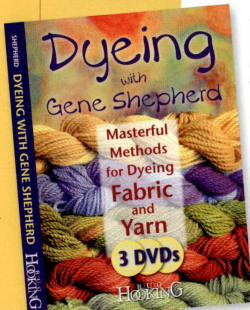

Dyeing with Gene Shepherd DVD Set
Learn from the master: watch as Gene Shepherd demonstrates his signature techniques. From dyeing with acid dyes to dyeing without dye, from dyeing wool fabric to dyeing yarn skeins and nylon, Gene covers it all. More than 4 hours of user-friendly instruction.
▲ Volume 1: Your Dye Kitchen; Equipment and Dyeing Basics
▲ Volume 2: How to Dye with Acid Dyes; Spots and Textures, Pots and Casseroles
▲ Volume 3: Dyeing Without Dye; Marrying and Marbleizing Colors

To see Gene in action and for a sneak peek of the videos, go to www.rughookingmagazine.com.
$17.95 each or $39.95 for the whole set

186　Prepared to Dye